RACE AND RECONCILIATION

Healing the Wounds,
Winning the Harvest

Jack W. Hayford
with
Greg Howse and Michael Posey

THOMAS NELSON PUBLISHERS
Nashville • Atlanta • London • Vancouver

CONTENTS

About the Executive Editor

JACK W. HAYFORD, noted pastor, teacher, writer, and composer, is the General Editor of the complete series, working with the publisher in the conceiving and developing of each of the books.

Dr. Hayford is Senior Pastor of The Church On The Way, the First Foursquare Church of Van Nuys, California. He and his wife, Anna, have four married children, all of whom are active in either pastoral ministry or vital church life. As General Editor of the *Spirit-Filled Life® Bible,* Pastor Hayford led a four-year project, which has resulted in the availability of one of today's most practical and popular study Bibles. He is author of more than twenty books, including *A Passion for Fullness, The Beauty of Spiritual Language, Rebuilding the Real You,* and *Prayer Is Invading the Impossible.* His musical compositions number over four hundred songs, including the widely sung "Majesty."

About the Writers

MICHAEL POSEY is the assistant pastor of Cornerstone Christian Center, a Foursquare Church in South Chicago Heights, Illinois, where he has served this multiethnic congregation for four years.

Michael has a zeal to help people realize their potential in life and to walk in their God-given calling. Michael is a bridge builder, bridging people to their dreams, and bridging the gap between the races to promote reconciliation. As a counselor, teacher, and speaker, Michael inspires the young and old alike to reach for their dreams and to answer destiny's call.

Michael and his wife Cathy have five children, Bryan, Marcus, Monica, Michelle, and Michael Jr.

GREG HOWSE is the pastor of Cornerstone Christian Center, a growing, multiethnic, cross-cultural Foursquare congregation in the south suburbs of Chicago, Illinois. He has been pastoring this local church since 1982. Cornerstone's constituency is African-American, Caucasian, and Hispanic/Latino.

Greg comes from a family of preachers. He graduated from U.C.L.A. in 1975 with a B.A. in Political Science. His ministry assignment is the facilitation of ethnic diversity and leadership development among pastors and local churches, the development of disciples, and church planting in the Chicagoland area. He is the author of two books, and he has written several magazine articles.

Greg and his wife Karen were married in 1979. They have two teenage children, Christine and Jonathan. Jonathan is Down's Syndrome, which has added to Greg and Karen's understanding of the handicaps many people face in life.

THE KEYS
THAT KEEP ON FREEING

Is there anything that holds more mystery or more genuine practicality than a key? The mystery: "What does it fit? What can it turn on? What might it open? What new discovery could be made? The practicality: Something *will* most certainly open to the possessor! Something *will* absolutely be found to unlock and allow a possibility otherwise obstructed!

- Keys describe the instruments we use to access or ignite.
- Keys describe the concepts that unleash mind-boggling possibilities.
- Keys describe the different structures of musical notes which allow variation and range.

Jesus spoke of keys: "And I will give you the keys of the kingdom of heaven, and whatever you bind on earth will be bound in heaven, and whatever you loose on earth will be loosed in heaven" (Matt. 16:19).

While there is no conclusive list of exactly what keys Jesus was referring to, it is clear that He did confer upon His church—upon *all* who believe—the access to a realm of spiritual partnership with Him in the dominion of His kingdom. Faithful students of the Word of God, moving in the practical grace and biblical wisdom of Holy Spirit-filled living and ministry, have noted some of the primary themes which undergird this order of "spiritual partnership" Christ offers. The "keys" are *concepts*—biblical themes that are traceable through the Scriptures and verifiably dynamic when applied with soundly based faith under the lordship of Jesus Christ. The "partnership" is the *essential* feature of this release of divine grace;

(1) believers reaching to *receive* Christ's promise of "kingdom keys," (2) while choosing to *believe* in the Holy Spirit's readiness to actuate their unleashing, unlimited power today.

Companioned with the Bible book studies in the *Spirit-Filled Life® Study Guide* series, the Kingdom Dynamic studies present a dozen different themes. This study series is an outgrowth of the Kingdom Dynamics themes included throughout the *Spirit-Filled Life® Bible,* which provide a treasury of insight developed by some of today's most respected Christian leaders. From that beginning, studious writers have evolved the elaborated studies you'll pursue here.

The central goal of the subjects focused on in this present series of study guides is to relate "power points" of the Holy Spirit-filled life. Assisting you in your discoveries are a number of helpful features. Each study guide has twelve to fourteen lessons, each arranged so you can plumb the depths or skim the surface, depending upon your needs and interests. The study guides contain major lesson features, each marked by a symbol and heading for easy identification.

  WORD WEALTH

The WORD WEALTH feature provides important definitions of key terms.

  BEHIND THE SCENES

BEHIND THE SCENES supplies information about cultural beliefs and practices, doctrinal disputes, business trades, and the like, that illuminate Bible passages and teachings.

AT A GLANCE

The AT A GLANCE feature uses maps and charts to identify places and simplify themes or positions.

KINGDOM EXTRA

Because this study guide focuses on a theme of the Bible, you will find a KINGDOM EXTRA feature that guides you into Bible dictionaries, Bible encyclopedias, and other resources that will enable you to glean more from the Bible's wealth on the topic if you want something extra.

PROBING THE DEPTHS

Another feature, PROBING THE DEPTHS, will explain controversial issues raised by particular lessons and cite Bible passages and other sources to which you can turn to help you come to your own conclusions.

FAITH ALIVE

Finally, each lesson contains a FAITH ALIVE feature. Here the focus is, So what? Given what the Bible says, what does it mean for my life? How can it impact my day-to-day needs, hurts, relationships, concerns, and whatever else is important to me? FAITH ALIVE will help you see and apply the practical relevance of God's literary gift.

As you'll see, these guides supply space for you to answer the study and life-application questions and exercises. You may, however, want to record all your answers, or just the overflow from your study or application, in a separate notebook or journal. This would be especially helpful if you think you'll dig into the KINGDOM EXTRA features. Because the exercises in this feature are optional and can be expanded as far as you want to take them, we have not allowed writing space for them in this study guide. So you may want to have a notebook or journal handy for recording your discoveries while working through to this feature's riches.

The Bible study method used in this series revolves around four basic steps: observation, interpretation, correlation, and application. Observation answers the question, What does the text say? Interpretation deals with, What does the text mean? —not with what it means to you or me, but what it meant to its original readers. Correlation asks, What light do other Scripture passages shed on this text? And application, the goal of Bible study, poses the question, How should my life change in response to the Holy Spirit's teaching of this text?

If you have used a Bible much before, you know that it comes in a variety of translations and paraphrases. Although you can use any of them with profit as you work through the *Spirit-Filled Life® Kingdom Dynamics Study Guide* series, when Bible passages or words are cited, you will find they are from the New King James Version of the Bible. Using this translation with this series will make your study easier, but it's certainly not necessary.

The only resources you need to complete and apply these study guides are a heart and mind open to the Holy Spirit, a prayerful attitude, and a pencil and a Bible. Of course, you may draw upon other sources, such as commentaries, dictionaries, encyclopedias, atlases, and concordances, and you'll even find some optional exercises that will guide you into these sources. But these are extras, not necessities. These study guides are comprehensive enough to give you all you need to gain a good, basic understanding of the Bible book being covered and how you can apply its themes and counsel to your life.

A word of warning, though. By itself, Bible study will not transform your life. It will not give you power, peace, joy, comfort, hope, and a number of other gifts God longs for you to unwrap and enjoy. Through Bible study, you will grow in your understanding of the Lord, His kingdom and your place in it, and those things are essential. But you need more. You need to rely on the Holy Spirit to guide your study and your application of the Bible's truths. He, Jesus promised, was sent to teach us "all things" (John 14:26; cf. 1 Cor. 2:13). So as you use this series to guide you through Scripture, bathe your study time in prayer, asking the Spirit of God to illuminate the text, enlighten your mind, humble your will, and comfort your heart. He will never let you down.

My prayer and goal for you is that as you unlock and begin to explore God's Book for living His way, the Holy Spirit will fill every fiber of your being with the joy and power God longs to give all His children. So read on. Be diligent. Stay open and submissive to Him. You will not be disappointed. He promises you!

Lesson 1/Blessed Are the Peacemakers

Greg Howse and Michael Posey

FEEL THE PAIN:

"The night has been long, the wound has been deep,
The pit has been dark, and the walls have been steep."[1]

FEEL THE PEACE:

"In His love no walls between us.
In His love, a common ground.
Kneeling at the cross of Jesus,
All our pride comes tumbling down.
Let the walls fall down . . .
By His love let the walls fall down."[2]

I (Greg) remember visiting in my office with several African-American couples who were new to our congregation during the last month of 1989. Each of them shared their story. Each of them told of frustration in trying to follow the call of God in their lives. Each of them reviewed their concerns for white and black issues within the body of Christ. Each of them expressed an undeniable hope in the purpose of God for their lives.

Each of them sat in my office and cried. And I cried with them—a white man, a white pastor, humbled that these men and women risked being transparent with me, humbled enough and motivated enough to respond in kind. I said something like this to each of them: "I don't understand fully what is happening here. I don't begin to know where this is going. But I want to help in whatever way I can. We can go somewhere together."

This study guide grew out of the years since then of intentional effort to come together across racial barriers as brothers and sisters in the name of Jesus. The starting point was a conviction that God isn't pleased with the division in His Son's body. Acting on that conviction led to transparency— often painful transparency—between men and women of different ethnic groups.

Stop and think for a minute. How have you seen the everyday racial tensions of your community make it uncomfortable for Christians to worship, serve, or live together?

Who do you know who is a Christian from another racial group? If you were having an honest talk about racial attitudes in the churches of your community, what would you want to know from him/her? (Remember this person is an individual, not a spokesman for "you people.")

THE INVITATION TO LIFE IN CHRIST

The call of God is an awesome thing in the life of a believer in Christ. It may be divided into two parts. The first calling is the invitation to enter life in Christ Jesus. The second calling is an appointment to ministry. Your understanding and depth of relationship in the first calling prepares you for the second calling.

Take note of the purpose of this first calling to life in Jesus in the following scriptures.

1 Peter 2:9

1 Thessalonians 4:7

1 Timothy 6:12

2 Timothy 1:9

Write your story of how you answered the invitation to enter life in Christ Jesus. You might want to write your story in three main paragraphs, according to the pattern Paul used in Acts 26:1–23.

• What was your life like before you met Jesus?

• How did you come to place your faith in Jesus?

• How has your life changed since you became a Christian?

Since you became a Christian, how has the Lord affected the way you treat people?

• Your family and friends

• Everyday contacts with strangers

• People you don't like

THE APPOINTMENT TO MINISTRY

This second part of the call of God on your life determines how your new life in Christ will contribute to the kingdom of God. God has shaped your personality by means of your family background and life experiences. The Holy Spirit has gifted you to contribute to the edification of Christ's body on earth. Your heavenly Father expects you to be listening for Him to direct you in expressing the unique ministry only you can have.

In several places in the New Testament, Paul wrote about his call to be an apostle to the Gentiles. Examine Paul's appointment to ministry as an example of how God expresses His call to others.

1. Rom. 1:1 Called to be an _____.

2. 1 Cor. 1:1; 2 Cor. 1:1 Called to be an _____

by the _____.

3. 1 Tim. 1:1 Called by the _____.

4. 2 Tim. 1:1 Called according to the _____ which is in

_____.

5. Titus 1:1 Called according to the _____

and the acknowledging of the _____ which is after

_____.

You are called/appointed according to God's purpose, not your talents or abilities. Your calling/appointment is something God decides, not you. This is not to say that your talents will not be put to use in your calling. But your talents do not determine your appointment.

Based on your understanding of God's work in your life, what do you think His appointment is for you?

What natural talents do you have that will help you fulfill your assignment?

What spiritual gifts do you have that will enable you to fulfill your assignment?

GREG HOWSE'S STORY

The writers of this study guide are pastors of Cornerstone Christian Center in South Chicago Heights, Illinois. Before you read and study further, meet the writers who are sharing their hearts and their insights gained through the pains and joys of spiritual warfare to see brothers and sisters in Jesus come together in love and respect across racial barriers.

"I was born in Los Angeles in 1952. When I was in the fifth grade my parents decided to move to Torrance. Their decision to move to the suburbs was based on the way our neighborhood in south-central L.A. was changing.

"Even though I grew up in a mostly white environment, I always had an interest in what was going on in the black culture. When I was a little boy, my dad served in the ministry with Aubrey Lee, who later pastored the Sky Pilot Church in south-central L.A. The director of the Sky Pilot Choir was Doris Akers. She would lead the choir as it marched down the aisles of that transformed movie theater singing "It's A Highway To Heaven." I remember André Crouch and the Disciples playing at local churches across southern California. Later I started playing piano in a group. One day an emerging new singer named Bill Withers came to one of our rehearsals. He pulled out his guitar and sang "Ain't No Sunshine When She's Gone."

"Nineteen sixty-eight was an amazing year. Martin Luther King, Jr. and Robert Kennedy were assassinated. Riots broke out as university students and other demonstrators protested at the Democratic convention in Chicago. But the biggest impression on me from that year originated from Mexico City. I was on my high school track team. I faithfully read the *Track and Field News.* Everything in those Olympic games was overshadowed by the black-glove salute of John Carlos and Tommie Smith on the victory stand. The media were waiting to see if Lee Evans would do the same thing after his victory in the 400 meters. He didn't. From then on Carlos and Smith were bad guys, while Evans was good.

"I was interested in the Black Panther Party and Angela Davis. I read *Soul On Ice* by Eldridge Cleaver and everything I could about the civil rights movement and its main leaders Martin Luther King, Jr., and Ralph Abernathy.

"Through all this I never had a black friend until I played the piano in a black Baptist church on L.A.'s south side during two of my college years. I made some good friends at that church. I also learned quite a bit about a culture different from my own. My final two college years were at U.C.L.A. I learned even more about cultural diversity there.

"All of these pieces of life have come together during the last several years of my pastoral ministry in the south suburbs of Chicago to reveal an image of God's purpose for my life. Since 1989 there has been a drastic cultural shift in our congregation. What was a 98% white church when I arrived in 1982 is now about 55% black, 35% white, and 10% Hispanic/Latino. Our

Christian school of 400 students has gone through a similar ethnic change.

"I enjoy a unique friendship with Michael Posey, a dear African-American brother who is the assistant pastor of our congregation and co-writer of this study guide. I have other solid relationships with members of the African-American culture that have served as vehicles of learning and maturity in my life and ministry. We are laboring to see many fine black young men and women come into their place of ministry. It has been a tremendous life-altering experience for me and my family. I would not trade it for any other ministry assignment in the world. God would have to pry me out of here.

"All of my unexplained interests and experiences in the early stages of my life were preparing me for my ministry assignment. Everything was "working together for good" because I love God and I am called according to His purpose (Rom. 8:28). My assignment is to bring God's people in our town together as an example to the world that people of ethnic and cultural diversity can function together in genuine love, true acceptance, and wonderful forgiveness."

MICHAEL POSEY'S STORY

"I was born on the south side of Chicago in 1961, and lived in the inner city for eighteen years. My mother and father separated before my first birthday and were later divorced. My older sister and I lived with my mother who did not marry again until I was ten years old. The neighborhood I grew up in was almost all black, except for the business owners who were either white or Arabic.

"My mother made a point of exposing me and my sister to the city outside our neighborhood. As far as I can remember race was never a major topic in our home. My parents and grandparents never talked negatively about people of different ethnic backgrounds, so I don't remember having any animosity toward different races. But I do remember, even as a child, a sense of pride and strength when we stopped referring to ourselves as 'colored' or 'negro' and said we were 'black.'

"In 1979 I joined the Marine Corps and much in my life changed. Two days before I was to leave for boot camp a good friend of mine brought over a guy that was already a Marine. We sat on my front porch and he began to tell me of how much discrimination was in the Corps. He recalled stories of how he and many other blacks were mistreated and denied promotions. I was eighteen. He scared me, and I thought about backing out. Today, I'm glad I joined the Marines, because the Lord used that period in my life to teach me much about people of different races.

"There was discrimination in the Corps, but I was sheltered from it my entire four years in the military. I worked with computers, and I was pretty good, so I didn't have many problems concerning my job. Now outside the work area, that was something else. In the military you have people from all over the country, and some had very definite views about blacks that I didn't agree with.

"One of the greatest things that happened to me in the Corps was the friendship I developed with Steve Wharton, a white guy from Downey, California. Steve and I met in boot camp and did our entire four years together. We were roommates much of the time and best friends more than that.

"We had much in common, and conversation was always easy for us. We learned a lot from each other. I watched the confidence Steve had about life and the future. By looking at him I started to change how I viewed my future. Steve talked matter-of-factly about one day buying a house. I hardly dared to dream that I would buy a house one day. It was what he took for granted for his future and what I only hoped for.

"Another thing that came from this relationship was Steve's loyalty to me. He would stand with me no matter what color the opposition was. At the time there weren't many blacks working computers in the Corps, so the majority of my unit was white. I wasn't the most outgoing man, and here I was spending all this time with whites. It wasn't always the most comfortable environment for me. With Steve's help I began to understand so much about the ignorance and fear that separate people of different races.

"When I returned home after my time in the Corps, I began working in data processing in the Sears corporate offices. I became very involved in my church. I had acquaintances of all races, but no significant relationships with anyone who wasn't black. I didn't feel any great desire to develop strong cross-cultural relationships. This changed when I walked through the doors of Cornerstone Christian Center. The congregation was predominantly white, but there was something about Pastor Greg Howse that I was drawn to.

"Greg and I began to get to know each other through an outreach ministry the church launched in the Ford Heights community. We started meeting one-on-one for discipling and accountability. After I attended the church for a little more than two years, Greg brought me on staff as assistant pastor of Cornerstone. Those years learning my way around the multiracial worlds of the Marine Corps and corporate America now make sense to me."

YOUR STORY

You are working your way through *Race and Reconciliation: Healing the Wounds, Winning the Harvest* because you have a sense that God is at work today to bring divided people in His church together in ways that will show His love and power to a world desperately in need of unity. Take a few minutes and reflect on what God may have in mind for you.

 FAITH ALIVE

Examine your own life experience. How have unexplained events and experiences in your life worked to develop you for the assignment God has for you?

How did your family background prepare you to deal with people?

What experiences and perspectives on life have you gained because of the places you have lived?

How would you describe your personality? How does it shape the way you relate to people?

What interests, natural abilities, and spiritual gifts affect your love for people and the ways you interact with them?

How has your education and work experience affected your skills in dealing with people?

 WORD WEALTH

Purpose translates a Greek word suggesting a deliberate plan, an intention, or a design. Most usages point to God's eternal purposes relating to salvation. Our personal salvation was not only well-planned but demonstrates God's abiding faithfulness as He awaits the consummation of His great plan for His church. God's purpose for your life is a piece of His overall cosmic purpose.[3]

Martin Luther King, Jr., said, "Man is man because he is free to operate within the framework of his destiny. He is free to deliberate, to make decisions, and to choose between alternatives."[4] What are some of the major choices you have made in life that have played major roles in shaping your life direction?

How would you explain God's ministry assignment for your life if you were talking to your closest friend?

What part do you think God has for you in the ministry of reconciliation (2 Cor. 5:18, 19)?

1. Excerpt from a poem by Maya Angelou, read at the "Million Man March," October 16, 1995.

2. Words and music by Bill Batstone, Anne Barbour, and John Barbour, © 1993 Maranatha! Music — Promise Keepers, '93, used by permission.

3. *Spirit-Filled Life® Bible* (Nashville: Thomas Nelson Publishers, 1991), 1701, "Word Wealth: Romans 8:28, purpose."

4. *Great Quotes from Great Leaders* (Lombard, IL: Celebrating Excellence Publishing, 1990), 12.

Part I
The Wall That Divides

The apostle Paul pictured humanity divided by walls of hostility (Eph. 2:14). He pictured the waist-high barrier in the temple courtyard in Jerusalem that separated gentile visitors from the areas where Jews could go.

Today, as in the first century, walls of suspicion divide the world into a crazy quilt of racial pride and rejection. Racial hatred is not fundamentally a problem of education, sociology, or politics. Racial hatred is fundamentally a spiritual problem. We will never face it and conquer it until we recognize its sinful character.

Lesson 2/Ethnic and Cultural Separation

Greg Howse

We live in a world in which billions of people are alienated from one another. This separation may be along the lines of age (old and young), economics (rich and poor), or sex (men and women). However, the most distinct and prominent rift is along ethnic and cultural lines. All one has to do is view one of the popular T.V. "talk" shows to witness alienation and hostility between various ethnic and cultural groups. The general reaction of whites and blacks to the verdict in the 1995 O.J. Simpson murder trial is another obvious measuring rod of the wide chasm between people groups.

Ethnic hostility is common all over the earth—from the Balkan struggle among the Serbs, Bosnians, and Croats, to the ethnic struggle within the United Kingdom, to the hostility between Israelis and Arabs in the Middle East, to the racial tension in South Africa, to the separation of Mexicans and Puerto Ricans in American cities. The most severe ethnic division in American society, and therefore, the one that has received the most attention, is the malevolent separation between whites and blacks.

 WORD WEALTH

Nation is the word for a race (as of the same habit), a tribe, or a foreign one—referring to a nation or people group. Even though the word "foreign" is used in this definition, an ethnic group should never simply be classified as "foreign ones." The word "ethnic" (from the Greek *ethnos,* i.e., nation) designates a population subgroup having a common cultural heritage distinguished by such things as national origin, customs, characteristics, language, and common history. The word "ethnicity" describes one's affiliation with a particular ethnic group.

THE UNITY OF THE HUMAN RACE

God's redemptive purpose includes bringing people together who have previously been divided. His redemptive plan stems from the fact that every ethnic group and culture come from one blood line, one set of parents, and one God. This truth from the Bible absolutely contradicts the humanistic, evolutionary philosophies of 20th century mankind. Let's take a look at the truth from the Word of God.

Acts 17:16–34 records Paul's ministry experience in the city of Athens. He preached what is arguably his most intellectual sermon on the Areopagus. Read this section of Scripture, especially focusing on verses 24–30.

Identify what you think is vital information about racial groups in Acts 17:26.

What should result from the way God allowed ethnic development to proceed? (Acts 17:27)

What did even the Greek philosophers and poets conclude about the diverse human race? (Acts 17:28)

As creatures of God, what should we conclude about the nature of God?

- Negatively (Acts 17:29)

- Positively (Acts 17:30)

God could have caused all descendants of Adam and Eve to remain ethnically alike. Why do you think He wanted His image to be reflected through widely divergent ethnic groups?

What do you think you learn about God, human nature, and yourself through close contacts with various racial groups?

- God

- Human nature

- Yourself

   KINGDOM EXTRA

In Acts 17:26 the unity of the human race is clearly stated, for through Adam and Eve (Gen. 3:20), and then the sons of Noah (Gen. 9:19), all races and nationalities of men came forth. We all proceed from one blood, both figuratively and literally, for the same blood types are found in all races. Humankind is a universal family (Mal. 2:10). We live in a single world community. No race or nation has the right to look down on or disassociate itself from another (Acts 10:28, 34, 35). There are only two divisions of humankind: the saved and the unsaved. Other differences are merely skin deep or culturally flavored, but all people are relatives.[1]

THE TOWER OF BABEL—THE PLACE OF ETHNIC SEPARATION

If all of us have our origin from the same earthly parents, how did we become so mixed up and divided? We find some clues to this perplexity in the story of the Tower of Babel, recorded in Genesis 11:1–9.

    BIBLE EXTRA

The city and kingdom of Babel was built and established by Nimrod. Nimrod was the son of Cush and the grandson of Noah (Gen. 10:8–12). His name is closely related to the Hebrew word *marad,* which means "to rebel," or "we will rebel." It points to open and violent rebellion against God. Genesis 10:9 says that Nimrod was a mighty hunter before the Lord. His hunting and mighty deeds were related to hunting men, as well as animals, by tyranny and force. "Before the Lord" suggests that his tyranny of men was done as an act of defiance against God. Nimrod was a city builder. It is said that he taught men to build walls around cities. These walls speak of *separation, defensiveness,* and *self-preservation.*[2]

What evidence of human pride exerting itself against God do you see in Genesis 11:4?

What did God say about the unity of the people in Genesis 11:6?

What was the first stage in scattering the people in Genesis 11:7–9? Why was this the most effective way to divide them?

How do you react to situations in which you cannot understand what people of another language group are saying?

When the united human race rose in proud defiance against God to make a name for itself, God withdrew His mighty, keeping hand from them. When God withdrew His hand there came a demonic visitation which initiated separation, alienation, and hostility. The confusion of languages was a manifestation of that demonic visitation.

 BEHIND THE SCENES

The ten languages spoken by the most people as their native tongue are as follows —

1. Chinese	840 million	6. Arabic	185 million
2. Hindi (Indian)	340 million	7. Russian	170 million
3. Spanish	335 million	8. Portuguese	170 million
4. English	325 million	9. Japanese	125 million
5. Bengali (Indian)	190 million	10. German	98 million[3]

This event at the Tower of Babel was not very long after the flood of Noah's time. The earth's population was still quite small. As each language group separated from the others and spread over the face of the earth, intermarriage and an intensifying gene pool within each group brought about the different skin pigmentations, facial features, and hair textures.

Why do you think superficial features such as skin color and hair texture cause us to react with caution and suspicion to one another?

If the Tower of Babel incident is the source of the tendency to withdraw from people unlike us, why should we expect that God would want His special people to resist and overcome that impulse?

THE DAY OF PENTECOST—A JOINING OF ETHNICITY FOR THE KINGDOM OF GOD

God specifically chose the feast of Pentecost as the time for the outpouring of His Spirit on His people. Acts 2:1–21 gives us a description of the happenings of that day. There are several striking contrasts between the Day of Pentecost and the incident at Babel.

Read Acts 2:1–21. Record the aspect of the Pentecost experience that counteracts the curse of Babel.

BABEL	PENTECOST
• Racial unity at first	•
• A visible human wonder	•
• Language confused	•
• People divided	•

At Pentecost the outpouring of the Spirit neutralized human separation. Where languages had been confused as a manifestation of demonic separation, the language of the Holy Spirit was given as evidence that the hearts of God's people were united in Christ Jesus. This language of the Spirit enabled a broadening of praise to the Lord, a widening path of intercession, a strategic opening in spiritual warfare, and a deeper intimacy in worship.

Why do you think nothing less than the powerful hand of God can reunite racial groups separated by centuries of mutual suspicion and mistreatment?

How do you think the Spirit-language of praise functions to overcome ethnic division and bond God's people into His community?

As mentioned earlier, God specifically chose Pentecost for this great event. There were Jews and proselytes from all over the known world in Jerusalem for the feast of Pentecost. Take note of all the places mentioned (vv. 9–11), and consult the map below to discover where these places were. Refer to a Bible dictionary or an encyclopedia and identify the modern country where each of these ancient locations is.

The Nations of Pentecost.[4]

Parthia_____   Phrygia _____

Media _____   Pamphylia _____

Elam _____   Egypt _____

Mesopotamia _____   Libya_____

Judea_____   Rome _____

Cappadocia_____   Crete_____

Pontus_____   Arabia _____

Asia _____

The Holy Spirit reversed what had happened at Babel by bringing people together in Christ Jesus. This was not legislated integration, but a willing acceptance of others in the heart of mankind. It was kingdom correctness instead of political correctness. It was love, acceptance, and forgiveness instead of mere toleration.

This Holy Spirit ministry of joining ethnicity spread from the ethnic and cultural representatives in Jerusalem to the far-reaching locations of the earth. We are accountable now to allow the Spirit to do what He set out to do on the day of Pentecost.

In your community, what groups feel uneasy with or distrustful of one another? Are they divided ethnically or by some other factor, such as economics, politics, or age?

How does the gospel of Jesus and the glory of Pentecost address the divisions in your community?

What can you imagine your church doing to minister in your community to help heal this division?

EXCLUSION AND INCLUSION

In New Testament times there was tremendous racial hatred between Jews and Gentiles and between various gentile races. The culturally proud Greeks regarded all non-Greeks as *barbaros.* Roman citizens considered themselves the only first-class people. True Romans—those native-born to one of Rome's seven hills—knew they were the *crème de la crème* of the earth. All slaves were subhuman.

Jews were thought to be weird. They had no visible god. Many Gentiles regarded them as atheists. Jews, of course, knew they were God's special people. Consequently, all Gentiles were despised by God. Then as now, each nation of the earth regarded its members as insiders with God or the gods, while all others were outsiders.

Read Ephesians 2:14–22 for a wonderful description of the joining of ethnicity for the Kingdom of God. Jesus is described in these verses as our peace. How does He provide peace between each of the following pairs?

• Hostile Jews and Gentiles (vv. 14, 15)

• Humans and God (vv. 16, 17)

Through the incarnation of Jesus, God experienced what it's like to be flesh. When His flesh endured crucifixion, Jesus annulled the Law that divided humanity into Jews and Gentiles (Eph. 2:15). How do His incarnation and crucifixion also provide the answer for the hostility between other racial groups?

What terms of exclusion do you find in verse 19? How do they express the hostility people often feel toward those of other races?

What terms of inclusion do you find in verses 19–22? How does each of them express an aspect of the harmony Christ died to create between born-again believers?

First Peter 2:4–10 describes the people who have come to Jesus to be made living stones in the spiritual house of God known as the church. In verse 9 believers are described as a generation which is _____, a priesthood which is _____, a nation which is _____, and a people which are _____.

First Peter 2:10 describes the people of this spiritual house of God as those who were not a people before they knew Jesus. No matter what our ethnic, racial, cultural, or nationalistic pride tells us, God says we were not a people before we knew Him. But now we are a people—the people of God. All the various ethnic and cultural groups which have been separated and alienated are brought together in Jesus Christ to become the people of God.

FAITH ALIVE

What is your ethnic or cultural background? How far back can you trace your family tree? How long has it grown in American soil?

How has your family kept its ethnic heritage alive or attempted to blend into the popular culture?

How does Peter's phrase "who once were not a people" (1 Pet. 2:10) apply to your ancestry? What emotional reactions do you have to such an expression?

How can you arrive at an accurate balance between being involved in and feeling good about your cultural heritage, and realizing that you were nothing before you met the Lord?

1. *Spirit-Filled Life® Bible* (Nashville: Thomas Nelson Publishers, 1991), 1661, "Kingdom Dynamics: Acts 17:26, The Unity of the Human Race."

2. *Dake's Annotated Reference Bible* (Lawrenceville, GA: Dake Bible Sales, Inc., 1963), 9, note on Gen. 10:8-11.

3. Andy Rooney in a segment of *60 Minutes* on C.B.S. (May 14, 1995).

4. *Spirit-Filled Life® Bible,* map on 1625.

Lesson 3/Ethnic and Cultural Idolatry

Greg Howse

Jason and Beth were a young couple of Scandinavian descent living in a southwestern city. Both of their families had been among the homesteaders in the territory, and they were proud of their local heritage. Their small children—a blond, blue-eyed boy and an equally fair girl—were replicas of every prior generation.

Jason and Beth belonged to a small Pentecostal church right in their neighborhood. They loved their pastor, their Christian friends, and the work of God in their lives there. Then the ethnic makeup of the congregation started changing as increasing numbers of aliens crossed the U.S.–Mexican border and settled in their city.

When their pastor spoke of looking for a Hispanic assistant, Jason and Beth realized their church really was going to be multiracial. Late one night they lay in bed talking about their children growing up in church with Mexican friends. They might date or marry Hispanics.

They began talking about leaving their church for a big church way out in the suburbs that had great children's programs. They didn't want it to look like they were leaving their home church because of the Mexicans. They loved all people with the love of the Lord. They merely wanted their kids to have a "safe place."

When a guest evangelist held renewal services at the church, a few unusual manifestations and biblical interpretations gave Jason and Beth the excuse they needed. They went to the pastor and explained that they could no longer worship there in good conscience.

The next day Beth was reading from Ephesians 2 during her morning devotions. She sensed the Holy Spirit dealing strongly with her heart that she and Jason were putting their blond hair and blue eyes ahead of the purpose of God for their lives and their church. That evening after tucking in the kids, she approached her husband. Tears ran down her cheeks as she told him what the Holy Spirit had revealed to her. He said he had been having similar thoughts about the situation. "What are we going to do?" Beth asked.

THE SIN OF IDOLATRY

The second and third commandments explicitly say that Israel was not to have any other gods before the true and living God (Ex. 20:3–6). They were never to make and worship any likeness of a created being. No creation of man could ever represent God. This conviction separated Israel from other nations who worshiped a multitude of gods represented in wood, stone, or precious metals.

Psalm 115:1–9 is an interesting commentary on the sin of idolatry. Verse 1 describes glory being given to the name of the Lord, instead of being directed toward anything that has to do with man. What are the reasons for glory being directed to the Lord's name?

Psalm 115:2 describes the nations looking for God in the form of an idol. Why do idolators have trouble relating to God being glorified by mercy and truth?

How is God portrayed in Psalm 115:3?

How are the physical characteristics of idols depicted in Psalm 115:4–7?

What does Psalm 115:8 say about those who make idols and put their trust in them?

In the New Testament, Paul referred to the wickedness of idolatry quite often. He told the Corinthian believers, "You were Gentiles carried away to these dumb idols, however you were led" (1 Cor. 12:3). By "dumb" Paul meant speechless, not stupid. If the idols could not speak, what "voices" were their worshipers hearing?

Paul told the Corinthians to test the various spirits by their attitude toward the lordship of Christ (1 Cor. 12:3). What are some ways people acknowledge that Jesus is Lord?

What are some ways people can curse the name of Jesus?

Read 1 Corinthians 12:4–13. Circle the letter of the following statement that you think best captures the message of these verses.
   a. You can tell whether you belong in the church by whether you have a spectacular spiritual gift.
   b. Dumb idols could never produce such a dynamic organism as the body of Christ.
   c. Everybody in the church should be the same.
   d. The Holy Spirit creates a unity that is displayed in a wide diversity.
   e. It's a liberal, impractical idea to expect different races to worship in the same church.

Why do you think we tend to feel more comfortable in groups of people made up of others just like us?

According to 1 Corinthians 12, why has God chosen to create the one, unified body of Christ with so much diversity among its many members? (See especially vv. 27, 28–30, 14, 18–25.)

 BEHIND THE SCENES

Webster defines idolatry as "excessive devotion or reverence for some person or thing." An idol is "any object of ardent or excessive devotion or admiration" or "a false notion or idea that causes errors in thinking or reasoning."[1] In this study guide the phrase *ethnic idolatry* means "a conscious or unconscious exaltation of personal racial or cultural concerns above the will of Christ for His church or for humanity as a whole." Ethnic idolatry curses Christ and refuses to submit to His lordship when He reaches across racial or cultural lines to create still greater unity out of still greater diversity.

Greek and Roman idolatry easily supplied every special interest group in society with a patron god or goddess to focus on. Paul did not want the church of Christ to fragment in the same way. What is it about ethnic idolatry that makes human effort inadequate and requires the Holy Spirit to break through the barriers among people this idolatry creates?

The following contemporary idols have no message from the Lord. They are "dumb" (1 Cor. 12:2). What messages from Satan does each of them inject into the life of a church that is affected by these idols?

- Absorption in materialism

- Absorption in work

- Absorption in politics

- Absorption in racial identity

THE DEMONIC NATURE OF IDOLATRY

Peter worked for IBM when he and Pam were introduced to a big-time direct sales company. Their all-white "upline" pushed them along saying, "We need successful blacks in this to prove you people can do it." In three years they built a third-level distributorship and enjoyed perks such as incentive trips to Hawaii. Then they were accused of illegal sales activities, and the company took away their "downline" business. Even after an investigation cleared them of all charges, management still sided with Peter and Pam's all-white accusers.

After the final crushing ruling, Peter found himself thinking: "You can't trust whites."

"They will backstab you as soon as they get a chance."

"A white person will only let you succeed to a certain point and then humiliate you."

Satan was challenging Peter to engage in a form of idolatry. The devil already had convinced the white businesspeople that race was god. Ethnic idolatry is common around the world, even in the church of Jesus Christ.

When Paul wanted to tell the Corinthians about Christian worship and spiritual gifts, he started with this statement: "Flee from idolatry" (10:14). First Corinthians 10 gives us several things to consider concerning idolatry. Verses 16–21 ask us to consider factors of identity.

In 1 Corinthians 10:16 and 17 how are believers identified with Christ?

With what was Israel identified? (1 Cor. 10:18)

With what do idolators identify? (1 Cor. 10:19, 20)

How do believers choose to identify with the Lord or demons? (1 Cor. 10:21)

 BIBLE EXTRA

Verse 21 teaches us that we must make a choice between devotion to the Lord or devotion to evil spirits. We enter a union with whatever or whomever has our devotion. Earlier in this same chapter Paul rehearsed the sins of Israel. Each point of sin had an evil spirit empowering it. *Idolatry* was empowered by *deception*. *Fornication* was empowered by *lust*. *Testing the Lord* was empowered by *arrogance*. *Murmuring* was empowered by *rejection* and *rebellion*.

WHEN ETHNICITY BECOMES IDOLATRY

Peter and Pam stopped attending their church because its pastor was white. Then one Sunday, Pam suggested they visit Cornerstone Christian Center. Peter had his reservations because he knew I was a white pastor. But co-writer Michael Posey was Peter's lifelong friend from the "hood." So Peter and Pam visited us, right on the Sunday that Michael was being appointed as the assistant pastor of the church. Peter still took the opportunity to pull Michael aside and warn him about me.

I don't think Peter had made his race an idol, but he was leaning in that direction. Unfortunately it does seem that the white sales managers who mistreated Peter had made their race something to protect and cherish. Most of us think that idolatry means pagan worshipers bowing before wood or metal images. But Caucasians can become immoderately devoted to the color of their skin in much more subtle ways than the extremist tendencies of white supremacist groups. Blacks may become immoderately devoted to various expressions of African culture.

Read the following Scriptures and record what each states or implies about how race or culture can become an idol.

• Luke 9:51–56

• Acts 10:44—11:18

• Galatians 2:11–18

Read the following Scriptures and record what each states or implies about what God has done regarding barriers between ethnic groups through Jesus Christ.

• Ephesians 2:11–17

• Colossians 3:9–11

• Revelation 7:9

To what racial group do you think God pays the most attention? Why do you tend to think that way?

Church growth experts tell us that the greatest movements of the Holy Spirit today are in Africa, Asia, and South America. What does this suggest about God's interest in skin color?

Historically, this idolatry has caused ethnic groups and cultures to conceive of God in their own image. If I am black and I want my biblical heroes to be black, I will manufacture every bit of evidence possible to prove my position to be accurate. If I am white I will insist on every biblical character fitting my Anglo-European perception no matter how historically, theologically, and scripturally unsound that is.

This inordinate devotion to skin color, culture, and ethnicity opens the door to demonic powers of pride, fear, racism, prejudice, bigotry, division, and hatred. These evil spirits feed on ignorance and stir hostility among people groups which God desires to bring together for His glory.

What do you think are the greatest contributors to racial idolatry among the residents of your community?

What are some things you and your church could be doing to eliminate or decrease racial prejudice and ignorance in your local community?

Some might say these demonic powers can only be destroyed through spiritual warfare. Others might say that practical, compassionate social programs in the neighborhoods are the answer. Other take a middle ground and say both are needed. How would you suggest battling racism in the church? Why do you take that position?

James 3:15 and 16 tells us that earthly wisdom is demonic, and that envy and self-seeking open the door for the entrance of confusion and every evil thing. How does this passage help explain the spiritual roots of ethnic and cultural idolatry?

 ## WORD WEALTH

Sensual (James 3:15) literally describes things that belong to the natural or physical realm of existence. To be sensual is to live in the domain of the five senses, concerned with this life only. Usually we use "sensual" to describe someone or something concerned with lusts, illicit desires, and unclean practices that open a person to the demonic.[2]

Self-seeking (James 3:16) translates a Greek adjective that regressed in meaning from denoting honorable work to suggesting dishonorable intrigue. Originally, it referred to a field-worker or reaper, and then anyone working for pay, a hireling. Later "self-seeking" described a person who was concerned only with his own welfare, a person susceptible to being bribed, an ambitious, self-willed person seeking opportunities for promotion. From there it became electioneering, a partisan factious spirit that would resort to any method for winning followers.[3]

How do you think ethnic and cultural idolatry fit the description of these two biblical terms?

• Sensual

• Self-seeking

According to Proverbs 13:10 and 28:25, what forces within the human soul are stirred up by pride?

How do you think this kind of pride contributes to ethnic and cultural idolatry?

 FAITH ALIVE

It is this cultural and ethnic pride which stirs our hostility toward one another. The judgment for this prideful idolatry is the same today as it has always been. There comes a visitation of the fathers' iniquity upon the children to the third and fourth generations. This visitation of iniquity comes to those who have made a choice against God (Ex. 20:5, 6).

How can the ethnic and cultural pride of preceding generations have a negative effect on you?

What can you do to stop the chain reaction of that iniquity in your generation?

THE WAY OUT OF IDOLATRY

Michael Posey invited Pam and Peter to attend a special meeting conducted at Cornerstone. The guest speaker gave very accurate personal words of knowledge as he ministered in a strong prophetic anointing. Kevin began to speak the "word of the Lord" to Peter. He told him he had run after the dollar and lost sight of God. He said, "Son, you will be a pillar in a church, and you must not go according to cultural matters, but go according to the realm of the Spirit." In receiving these words, Peter's hurt and disillusionment immediately dissolved. That prophetic word also caused Peter to evaluate me as a pastor on the basis of my anointing by the Holy Spirit rather than my skin color.

When God convicts us of the sin of ethnic or cultural idolatry, how might we need to repent (change) in each of these areas?

- Thinking

- Perception

- Speech

- Behavior

How does the Lord Jesus empower us to repent of attitudes and behaviors that separate believers in Jesus along racial and cultural lines? (Eph. 2:14, 15)

What do you think the Lord expects His followers to find when the walls of racial division come down that we can discover no other way?

 FAITH ALIVE

In the following quotation replace the words, "Jew and Gentile," with the two (or more) ethnic groups that are most alienated in your community. "For He is [Himself] our peace (our bond of unity and harmony). He has made us both

[   ]

one [body], and has broken down (destroyed, abolished) the hostile dividing wall between us" (Eph. 2:14, Amplified Bible).

How do you think Jesus expects us to express in practical terms the reconciliation He accomplished on the cross?

1. *Webster's New World Dictionary* (New York: Simon and Schuster, 1988).

2. *Spirit-Filled Life® Bible* (Nashville: Thomas Nelson Publishers, 1991), 1899, "Word Wealth: James 3:15, sensual."

3. Ibid., 1802, "Word Wealth: Phil. 1:16, selfish ambition."

Lesson 4/The Rainbow Reaches The Suburbs

Greg Howse

Daniel was an African-American boy growing up in the inner city of Chicago during the late sixties. Even though he lived in the inner city, his father wanted to make sure that the inner city did not live in Daniel. The father's goal was to show Daniel and his seven siblings that there was a bigger world beyond their neighborhood in Chicago. Every year Daniel's father took the family on an extended camping trip somewhere in the United States. Daniel was always proud to place on their camper a sticker of another state visited.

Even when he was in grade school Daniel knew something was different about his family. They were always the only African-Americans in the campground, no matter where they traveled. Daniel does not remember any overt acts of racism, but it always fascinated him to be playing with all black kids one week and then all white kids for the next three.

Daniel considered his family vacations a positive experience because his father never allowed the family to look at themselves as a black family invading a white person's world. They were just an American family enjoying a summer vacation with other American families.

SEPARATION IN OUR URBAN CENTERS

"BATTLEGROUND CHICAGO: The Germans and the Irish came first. Then the Italians and the Poles. White ethnics

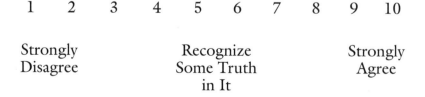

were Chicago, really. They walked the beat, collected the trash, built the city. But Chicago's most controversial migration happened later, during and after World War II. Hundreds of thousands of Southern blacks, fleeing enforced segregation, moved in. And Chicago, after absorbing so many other newcomers, resisted. The stage, familiar in cities both North and South, was set: standoffish whites and shut-out blacks."[1]

The last phrase in that quotation from *Newsweek* is crucial for our understanding of ethnic, racial, and cultural separation—"standoffish whites and shut-out blacks." As blacks and other minorities have moved into the larger American cities, whites have set themselves in a standoffish mindset, consciously or unconsciously protecting their predominant piece of the American pie we call success. Whites eventually began leaving the city for the more comfortable, serene atmosphere of the suburbs. Now we are faced with the tragedy of the inner city in America.

Who are the primary ethnic minorities in your community?

How would you assess the attitudes of your community toward each of these ethnic minorities?

On the following scale, rate your opinion of the phrase "standoffish whites and shut-out blacks" as descriptive of your community.

1	2	3	4	5	6	7	8	9	10

Strongly   Recognize   Strongly
Disagree   Some Truth   Agree
                                in It

Explain why you chose the rating you did.

 BEHIND THE SCENES

Consider the following statistics.
- Homicide is the leading cause of death for black males and females ages fifteen to thirty-four.[2]
- Blacks account for 44% of all homicide victims, even though they make up only 12% of the population.[3]
- 99% of black homicides were committed by black perpetrators.[4]
- Infant mortality among blacks is twice as high as for white infants.[5]
- In the ten largest urban centers, the high school dropout rate for black males is 72%.[6]
- The 1991 unemployment rate for black Americans was 12.9%—more than twice the rate for white Americans.[7]
- At the end of the 1980s, more than half of the African-American children were born to single mothers.[8]
- In 1960, 78% of black families with children were headed by both a mother and a father—a figure that dropped to 37% by 1990.[9]

How do these statistics make you feel about the plight of our inner cities?

What would be some helpful responses of the church of Jesus Christ to this information?

The *Chicago Tribune* ran a series in the fall of 1994 entitled, "The Graying of Suburbia." Louis Masotti of U.C. Irvine wrote, "Just like people go through phases in their life-cycle, cities go through phases. Some can no longer be what they once were. I think the inner-ring suburbs are much more like the central city than the next ring of suburbs. The problems of the city have suburbanized."[10]

The inner-ring suburbs are the band around the city that in places stretches ten miles or more outward. They are "mature communities," distinct from those farther out. People are moving out of this inner-ring for a variety of reasons. Some move to keep their jobs as their companies move. Some see that housing values have peaked and are on the decline. They see racial or class change as imminent. And they see the school systems faltering.

Suburbanites keep moving farther out from the city because they want a new house, good schools, good jobs in a safe area, safe streets, an acre lot, a three-car garage, and a big deck for entertaining. Some want to avoid contact with other races.

The popular term for this migration to the outer-ring suburbs is "suburban sprawl." This is very worrisome for city officials who see money fleeing from the aging inner-ring communities for the trendy, wide-open spaces of the outer-ring suburbs.

What are the exclusive neighborhoods in or around your community where people move to escape urban problems?

What do you think are the best arguments for moving away from the heart of town?

What do you think are the best arguments for staying close to downtown?

What do you think are the greatest problems faced by churches that serve the Lord in the inner city?

How do you think churches in the outer-ring suburbs could minister in partnership with inner-ring or inner-city churches to help them deal with the deepening needs of their communities?

Kenneth Jackson of Columbia University observes, "In the United States we're a people rich in land and resources, so we've thrown away communities like Pepsi cans. It's a process seen over the last century and a half in urban areas. Now it's reached to the inner suburbs and is moving beyond them. The only thing that's new is its moving outside the city."[11]

Do you agree or disagree with Jackson that we are abandoning life in our cities and towns too quickly to escape urban problems? Explain your answer.

How do you think you would recognize the leading of God if He wanted you and your family to serve Him in a city as a salt and light to slow or reverse the decay?

 KINGDOM EXTRA

In Numbers 13:1—14:45 Joshua and Caleb resisted the report of the ten spies who were afraid to obey the Lord because invading Canaan looked too difficult. Unbelief looks at obstacles; faith looks at God. Joshua and Caleb were willing to do the unpopular thing and call the people to positive faith. They led the way into the future by confronting a negative report and helping a new generation rise to serve God in faith.[12]

How can you rise up as a "Joshua" in your community, and encourage God's people to resist the popular opinion that giving up on towns and cities is the smart thing to do?

What churches in your area have moved out of town? Why did they move?

What kinds of churches serve your downtown? Are they spiritually healthy?

What ministry opportunities would a downtown church have in your community that a suburban or rural church doesn't have?

 FAITH ALIVE

Why have you chosen to live where you do: inner city, inner-ring suburb, outer-ring suburb, or in a rural area?

What are your images and impressions of the inner-city?

Are your feelings based on experience, what you have seen in the media, or what you have heard from others?

What role do you think each of the following should play in restoring our inner cities?

• Government

• Business

• Private enterprise

• The church

Acts 1:8 is a mandate from the Lord Jesus to be witnesses to Him, starting at home and moving progressively farther out until the entire earth has received this witness. Your Jerusalem could be an outer-ring suburb or the inner city. It is your comfort zone.

Judea is a place that is slightly different geographically, but is culturally the same as your Jerusalem. Move on to your Samaria, a place that may be geographically close but culturally different. If Jerusalem is an inner city, Samaria could be an outer-ring suburb, or vice versa. Now we are being stretched. From Samaria we go to the ends of the earth, the nations.

An interesting phenomena is that the nations are coming to our major inner-cities. For many of us, going to the ends of the earth may be a call to go back to the inner-city to meet the nations face to face.

What nations are represented in the urban center that is closest to you?

What would be some creative ways of reaching those ethnic groups with the gospel?

BEHIND THE SCENES

In an article entitled, "A New Look At America," *Time* reported the following information about foreign-born people groups living in American urban centers.[13]

- More than 100 languages are spoken in the school systems of New York City, Chicago, Los Angeles, and Fairfax County, Virginia.
- 32 million people in the U.S. (13%) speak languages other than English at home.
- In 1940, 70% of immigrants came from Europe. In 1992, 15% came from Europe, 37% from Asia, and 44% from Latin America and the Caribbean.
- American cities where more than half the population is foreign born —

Hialeah, FL—70%	Union City, NJ—55%
Miami, FL—60%	Monterey Park, CA—52%
Huntington Park, CA—59%	Miami Beach, FL—51%

What do these statistics suggest about outreach opportunities in our urban centers?

How could your local church effectively respond to these needs?

How could your church interact with ethnic churches in the nearest urban center in each of these areas?

- Worship

- Evangelism

- Youth activities

• Missions opportunities

KINGDOM EXTRA

In teaching kingdom life and principles, Jesus leads His followers to think, live, and pray that His kingdom come to our entire planet (Matt. 6:10). In Matthew 13, His parables illustrated the kingdom's global expansion. As His disciples began to minister, He told them to preach *everywhere:* "The kingdom of God is at hand." Then, before His ascension, the King gave the Great Commission. This climaxing command to go to all nations directed that their teaching and preaching seek to bring all nations into His kingdom (Matt. 28:18–20). Prophetically, He forecast that the end would come only as "this gospel of the kingdom" was preached "in all the world as a witness to all nations" (Matt. 24:14). "Nations" means "people groupings"—today, about 22,000 on this globe.[14]

How does the aim of this "Great Commission" ("all the nations") apply to reaching people in our inner cities and suburbs?

How could you have a ministry to an individual or group of people who came from another country?

FAITH ALIVE

How would you describe your "Jerusalem" comfort zone?

How far away is your "Samaria" and who are the people who live there?

What are the natural points of hostility between your culture and that culture? How can you demonstrate your willingness to break down the walls of separation?

What is your inner response to the idea that God might call you to cross borders and go to other nations in the inner city?

1. "Battleground Chicago," *Newsweek* (CXXV, 13), 26.

2. Carl C. Bell, "Preventing Black Homicide," *The State of Black America 1990* (New York: National Urban League, 1990), 143-145.

3. Ibid.

4. Ibid.

5. La Salle D. Leffall, Jr., "Health Status of Black Americans," *The State of Black America 1990*, 131.

6. Mark S. Hoffman, ed., *The World Almanac* (New York: Paros, 1992), 162.

7. Marvin McMickel, "Black Men: Endangered Species," *Club-Date* (Aug./Sept. 1989), 29.

8. Andrew W. Edwards, "The Black Family: A Unique Social System in Transition," *The State of Black Cleveland 1989* (Cleveland: Urban League of Greater Cleveland, 1989), 187.

9. Andrew Billingsley, "Understanding African-American Family Diversity," *The State of Black America 1990*, 89, 90.

10. Laurie Goering, "The Graying of Suburbia," *The Chicago Tribune* (September 4, 1994), sec. 1, p. 6.

11. Ibid.

12. *Spirit-Filled Life® Bible* (Nashville: Thomas Nelson Publishers, 1991), 212, "Kingdom Dynamics: Numbers 13:1—14:45, Resisting Popular Opinion."

13. "The Numbers Game," *Time Magazine Special Issue* (Fall 1993), 14-15.

14. Ibid., 1464, "Kingdom Dynamics: Matthew 28:18-20, Commissioned Under the King's Call."

Part II
The Tie That Binds

We sing that old hymn, "Blest Be the Tie That Binds," without asking often what that tie is. In the first verse it is identified as "the fellowship of kindred minds." The longer we walk with the Lord Jesus under the leadership of the Spirit of God, the more we understand that the fellowship of kindred minds has little, if anything, to do with similarities in economic status, educational background, or national origin.

The preceding chapters focused on the spiritual forces that try to divide the body of Christ along ethnic lines. The response to these forces must primarily be spiritual as well. Jesus is the great Reconciler. The Holy Spirit is the great Comforter. The church is God's great new creation in which all men are made new and made one in Christ. No human organization will ever do what the church can do to unite the divided. As much as it depends on our obedience, let's be sure the church does what it must.

Lesson 5/Who Can Heal The Wounds?

Greg Howse

Jeanette is an African-American, single parent who attends Cornerstone Christian Center. Not too long ago, she purchased a house in Forest Park, a nearby racially-mixed village. Every day she felt like pinching herself to see if this pretty little house was a dream. Then the anonymous letter from a neighbor appeared in her mailbox. "Your kind will only depreciate the value of our property."

Instantly, a cloud blocked the sun of Jeanette's joy. She could have withdrawn into her house behind locked doors. She could have withdrawn into herself behind locked doors of anger and bitterness. Instead Jeanette approached her problem as a spiritual challenge. She prayed for her neighbor—whichever one it was—so that her heart would stay pure and forgiving. She also set out to make her house and yard the best on her block.

First some elderly Caucasian neighbors complimented her for keeping such a beautiful home. They were glad to see her house brighten theirs. Finally Jeanette met the neighbor who wrote the letter when he came over and apologized to her. The cloud lifted. Her new neighborhood was a joy again.

THE NEED FOR RECONCILIATION

Jeanette's experience is exceptional—exceptional because she refused to respond to hatred with hatred. She overcame evil with good (Rom. 12:21). Even if her hostile neighbor had never voiced his repentance, she would have heaped "coals of fire on his head" (v. 20) and made him feel like a heel. Because he let go of his hostility, he and Jeanette experienced a measure of reconciliation. At this time, only God knows how much.

Circle the letter of the response that best expresses your attitude toward what Jeanette did.

    a. Jeanette is an exception. Nobody should change their opinions based on exceptions.

    b. Jeanette was a good neighbor, but you have to make property decisions based on cold, hard realities.

    c. I would like to do the right thing about interracial neighborhoods, but I'm afraid of losing my investment.

    d. I admire Jeanette. I'd live in an interracial neighborhood with neighbors like that.

    e. Jeanette shouldn't have to be a saint and a martyr to buy a house and have friends.

    f. I don't think Jeanette should have forgiven the letter writer so quickly.

What responsibilities do you think Christians have to be peacemakers in neighborhoods having their first experiences with racial integration?

FAITH ALIVE

Most of our racial attitudes spring from our childhood experiences with our parents, church leaders, teachers, and other key adults. Think for a minute about the way you were raised from childhood to adulthood. Consider the experiences you had with people from other ethnic groups or cultures. How does your background cause you to react to these key concepts of racial alienation?

• Prejudice

• Fear

• Ignorance

• Acceptance

• Trust

Reconciliation Through Jesus Christ

Second Corinthians 5:14–21 teaches us that God was in Christ Jesus reconciling the world unto Himself. The Lord Himself is the supreme example of reconciliation. We were fearful of exposure to His presence. We were ignorant of His purpose in the earth. We were alienated from Him by our sin. We refused to accept Him because of our rebellion against Him. We refused to trust Him. We were suspicious of Him.

But He loved us unconditionally, and His love motivated Him to make a move toward us. He came to us as a man, full of grace and truth. We need to be confronted with His truth. We need to be supported and empowered by His grace.

Now it is up to us to imitate our Lord and make a radical move toward those who are alienated from us. As we are reconciled we overcome fear, ignorance, alienation, and hostility through the power of relationship. The love of Christ compels us to make this move.

How will our racial relations be affected if "we regard no one according to the flesh"—that is, refuse to judge by worldly, human standards? (2 Cor. 5:16)

What aspects of racial hostility do you think are among the "old things" that pass away when we are reconciled to Christ? (2 Cor. 5:17)

If we are ambassadors urging people to be reconciled to God through Christ, how should our ministry of reconciliation affect relationships between Christians of different races? (2 Cor. 5:18–21)

WORD WEALTH

Compels (2 Cor. 5:14) translates a compound Greek verb meaning "to hold together," or "to grip tightly." In every use of the word, there is a sense of constraint, a tight grip that prevents escape. The love of Christ leaves us no choice except to live our lives for Him. That love gets downright pushy when its compulsion involves reconciling alienated people.[1]

When have you felt compelled by the love of Christ to reach out to someone you ordinarily would have ignored or avoided?

If the love of Christ were going to compel you to be reconciled with a brother or sister of another race, what would be the greatest barrier in the way of His love?

AT A GLANCE

2 Cor. 5:	What is the radical concept?	How does this concept apply to you?
14, 15	A radical love	He died for us so we live for Him.
16	A radical perception	We regard no one according to the flesh.
17	A radical change	Old things have passed away; all things have become new.
18	A radical ministry	The ministry of reconciliation.
19	Radical ambassadors	The word of reconciliation is committed to us.

When we were reconciled to God, He didn't change. Only we did. What had to change for us to be reconciled to Him?

When we are reconciled to other people, usually both human parties have to change. Neither is perfect. What do you think has to change for people of different races or cultures to be reconciled to one another?

When both parties need to change in order for reconciliation to occur, often each waits for the other to change first. Who do you think the Lord expects to take the initiative in racial reconciliation? Why?

PROBING THE DEPTHS

"But all things are from God, Who through Jesus Christ reconciled us to Himself [received us into favor, brought us into harmony with Himself] and gave to us the ministry of reconciliation [that by word and deed we might aim to bring others into harmony with Him]."

(2 Cor. 5:18 AMPLIFIED)

Reconciliation has a twofold reality.
1. It has already happened (with God). God has already brought us into favor and harmony with Himself.
2. It is still in progress (with us). We aim to bring others into favor and harmony with the Lord. We illustrate this by the favor and harmony we have with one another as fellow Christians.

How has God changed you so you can enjoy greater favor and harmony with Him?

How does God need to change you so you can enjoy greater favor and harmony with brothers and sisters in Christ from other racial and cultural groups?

   WORD WEALTH

Reconciled (1 Cor. 7:11) is the past participle of a verb meaning "to change," "to restore a relationship," or "to make things right." This word describes the reestablishing of a proper, loving, interpersonal relationship, which has been broken or disrupted.[2]

WE ARE CALLED TO BE RECONCILERS

Second Corinthians 5:20 tells us that we are ambassadors for Christ, as though God were pleading through us. God, who reconciled the world to Himself through the death of His Son, is now inviting the world, through His ambassadors, to be reconciled to Him. To be ambassadors for Christ is to be reconcilers wherever relationships are broken.

The apostle Paul worked for years to promote reconciliation in Christ between Jews and Gentiles. Until recently, there hasn't been much organized concern among Bible-believing Christians about racial separation in the church. Why do you think we have been slow to promote reconciliation among Christians of different races and cultures?

Why do you think God has been impressing the need for racial reconciliation on the hearts of so many conservative church leaders and laypeople?

What do you think Bible-centered and Spirit-centered racial reconciliation has to offer our divided communities that liberal Christianity never can?

 WORD WEALTH

Ambassador (Eph. 6:20) literally meant "to be an elder." Later it took on the governmental sense of a representative of the ruling authority. Ambassadors were chosen from the ranks of mature, experienced men. To be an ambassador for Christ, representing Him on the mission of reconciliation in all of its dimensions, necessitates advanced spiritual maturity.[3]

This work of reconciliation is centered in Jesus Himself (Eph. 2:14, 15). He is our peace and He is also our peacemaker. There are not many people groups in Christ, there is only one—those who have been washed in the blood of Jesus. Through His cross He brought us all together, destroying hostility, recreating us as one new man. He did not bring other ethnic groups up to the level of the best group. That would lead to one race claiming to be the super-ethnic group. Instead He produced a supra-ethnic group—His church!

What do you think are the factors that lead to feelings of racial enmity in your community?

How does the cross of Jesus Christ address those factors and provide a basis for peace between the races?

What do you think churches and individual Christians will have to do in your community to deal with racial enmity there?

BIBLE EXTRA

Josephus used the term "middle wall" (Eph. 2:14) to describe the partition that separated the court of the Gentiles from the main part of the temple in Jerusalem. The inscription on the partition said, "No Foreigner may enter within the barricade which surrounds the sanctuary and enclosure. Anyone caught doing so will have himself to blame for his ensuing death."[4]

Even though Ephesians 2:14 is focusing on Jew and Gentile, give consideration to current people groups which have a middle wall of separation. How can the principle "He Himself is our peace" work for these groups also?

The Lord aims to create in Himself one new man from two, thus making peace. How can this be facilitated between hostile, alienated ethnic groups today?

When Paul tried to capture the ferocity of the mutual racial hostility between Jews and Gentiles, he said they looked at one another as "strangers" and "foreigners" (Eph. 2:19). These labels identified people of inferior status. Paul stated, in no uncertain terms, that these who were thought of as inferior had all the privileges of the household of God through union with Christ.

What are some practical ways we can remind ourselves that Christians from other ethnic groups are full citizens of the same kingdom we belong to?

We are being built together to become a dwelling place for God's presence (Eph. 2:22). This building consists of every kind of people on planet earth. The key is that we are "being built together." We are aligned with the cornerstone, Christ Jesus.

- Write down the words in Ephesians 2:19 which are exclusionary.

- Write down the words in this Scripture which are inclusionary.

- What are some of the things we do that exclude Christians of other races from our fellowship?

• What do we need to do to include Christians of other races in our fellowship?

"There is no distinction between Greek and Jew [or any other diverse groups which would tend to be divided by hostility], . . . but Christ is all, and in all" (Col. 3:11, NASB).

We like to make distinctions between groups of people, especially when our group feels hostile to the other. But there is no distinction when we are in Christ. Certainly there is, and always will be, diversity in the body of Christ. But this diversity is never to serve as a barrier to fellowship; it is never to be an instrument of threat or intimidation. Our diversity should serve as a complimenting factor for an example to the world. Jesus Christ is the great principle of all true unity. Loyalty to Jesus must be our priority over all natural earthly ties.

If you could suggest one activity this year for your church to promote greater harmony and cooperation among Christians of different races, what would you like to see happen?

What could you do to increase the likelihood that this will happen?

1. *Spirit-Filled Life® Bible* (Nashville: Thomas Nelson Publishers, 1991), 1758, "Word Wealth: 2 Cor. 5:14, compels."

2. Ibid., 172, "Word Wealth: 1 Cor. 7:11, reconciled."

3. Ibid., 1797, "Word Wealth: Eph. 6:20, ambassador."

4. A. Skevington Woods, "Ephesians," *The Expositor's Bible Commentary*, Vol. 11 (Grand Rapids, MI: Zondervan Publishing House, 1978), 40.

Lesson 6/The Church Jesus Died to Start

Greg Howse

"Hyphenated, intermarrying, and increasingly blended people—and we are likely to become both more diverse, and more nearly like each other, as time goes by."[1] That was the description of Americans given in the May 18, 1992, issue of *Newsweek,* following the riots in L.A. after the Rodney King verdict. The same article went on to describe the vast diversity of nationalities and ethnic groups in the greater Los Angeles area.

The interesting thing about this mixture of people groups in Los Angeles is that it characterizes most major U.S. cities. Furthermore, it is becoming increasingly characteristic of many mid-size cities and towns across the country. A growing percentage of our communities are becoming more diverse, and in this strange fashion we are becoming more like each other.

THE IMPORTANCE OF CROSSING CULTURES

God has sovereignly placed His church in the midst of all this and commands us to preach the gospel to every creature, making disciples of every ethnic group. He is raising up a new breed of pastoral leaders who are intentional about loving and accepting people of diverse ethnic heritages. These trailblazers have discovered ways and means of bridging the gaps between cultures. People of various ethnic backgrounds recognize in these leaders the unifying love and acceptance of Jesus.

List some of the character traits and abilities you think a leader needs to cause people to recognize Christ at work in him or her.

What character traits and leadership abilities do you have that could foster a cross-cultural ministry?

What character traits and leadership abilities do you have that make you a good follower for a godly leader in a cross-cultural ministry?

My family and I moved from Waterloo, Iowa, to Chicago Heights in August of 1982. We came to pastor Cornerstone Christian Center, a Foursquare church that was Caucasian, with the exception of one Mexican family. Our first black family came to the church that October. They were the only black family in the church for years. Then toward the end of 1989, as I mentioned in chapter 1, many black brothers and sisters started coming, one family after another. We weren't doing anything differently from the way we had always done things. It just started happening.

Through the intervening years, the Lord has seen fit to gather a racially mixed congregation, approximately 55% black, 35% white, and 10% Latino. I often tell people that our church is not a black church or a white church or a Hispanic church; it is God's church. It is a church that Jesus died for.

In Acts 10:34 and 35, Peter said, "In truth I perceive that God shows no partiality. But in every nation whoever fears Him and works righteousness is accepted by Him."

Read Acts 10:1–33. What kind of partiality had Peter been trained all his life to show to other people?

How easy/difficult did Peter find it to overcome his partialities? (See also Gal. 2:11–14.)

 WORD WEALTH

Partiality (Acts 10:34) translates a Greek word which literally meant "a receiver of a face." From that colorful meaning emerged the idea of "putting on a face of preference," "taking sides," and "showing favoritism." While fallen human society specializes in **partiality** among people, God makes His love and grace available for all. He has only one face, and He shows that same face to all people.[2]

How do favoritism and bias show up in our churches?

What hidden problems in a church do you think would be exposed if someone openly challenged its partiality?

What are some things your church could do to make God's grace and love available to people of all ethnic and cultural groups who might visit or attend it?

What can you do personally to make your church a more accepting place for visitors of another race?

THE IMPORTANCE OF RELATIONSHIP AND COMMUNICATION

When Cornerstone Christian Center began to go through its cultural transformation, my wife and I started an ongoing conversation with black brothers and sisters. We continue to learn much from their perspective on life and ministry. I hope they in turn have gained from us.

We have often discussed the nitty-gritty issues of racism. Hidden prejudices, fears, and inaccurate perceptions have been uncovered and dealt with. Acceptance and intimacy only come through a willingness to relate with one another.

John 17:22–24 makes it clear that any godly relationship must be modeled on the relationship between God the Father and Jesus the Son. Verse 24 tells us that a relationship between God as Father and Jesus as Son preceded our relationship with Them. Verse 23 tells us that the Father's commitment to relationship is first to Jesus and then along the same lines to us. Verse 22 describes a network of committed relationships among the Father, the Son, the Spirit, and all believers.

What practical issues make unity among all believers difficult to achieve?

What sinful attitudes that some believers don't want to repent of also hinder unity within the worldwide church?

The world tends to sort people through social screening processes into groups that are alike—clubs, occupations, special interest groups. On what basis does God expect Christians to override ordinary social conventions and find unity with people of different races and cultures?

The apostle John wrote that everything he did in ministry was aimed at the development of relationships (1 John 1:3–7). He was sharing his experience in the gospel to open new doors of fellowship. As we walk in the light we give evidence of our fellowship with the Lord and our relationship with one another. The life of fellowship is a life that is continually cleansed from sin by the blood of Jesus.

How do you think the gospel of Christ functions as a uniting mechanism to establish fellowship between people who would not be friends in the flesh?

What effect do you think walking in the darkness of racial prejudice and hatred has on a Christian's relationship in the light with the Father and the Son?

    WORD WEALTH

Fellowship (Acts 2:42) is a many-sided term meaning all of the following: sharing, unity, close association, partnership, participation, a society, a communion, a fellowship, contributory help, the brotherhood. Fellowship is unity brought about by the Holy Spirit. In such *koinonia* the individual shares in common an intimate bond of fellowship with the rest of the Christian society. It cements believers of all races to the Lord Jesus and to each other.[3]

First John 4:7–21 gives us a pattern for loving relationships. As mentioned in chapter 2, the New Testament world was full of bigotry. The Romans thought the Greeks were effeminate intellectuals. The Greeks thought the Romans were bullies trying to buy or steal culture. Greeks and Romans thought all Asians were crooked merchants. Everybody thought the Jews held dangerous religious views. Not to be outdone, the Jews despised all Gentiles as (yuck!) Gentiles.

First John 4:7–21 is a beautiful message about love for a world that experienced little of it. Look up the following passages and write down the indicated aspect of love.

- (1 John 4:7) The foundation for love.

- (1 John 4:8) God and love.

- (1 John 4:9, 10) How God's love works.

- (1 John 4:11) God's love and ours.

- (1 John 4:12) Showing God to the world.

- (1 John 4:13–19) Love and confident ministry.

- (1 John 4:20) Lying "love."

- (1 John 4:21) The unity of love.

Based on 1 John 4:7–21, how would you say each member of the Trinity contributes to the love we should have for Christians of all races and cultures?

- The Father

- The Son

- The Holy Spirit

What will happen to our ability to love believers of other races if we let the spirit of fear control our hearts and minds? (1 John 4:17, 18)

What will happen to our racial and cultural fears if we let the spirit of love control our hearts and minds? (1 John 4:17, 18)

In the Chicago area—as in much of the rest of the country—there are several large, racially-mixed congregations which are led by Caucasian pastors and leadership. In those situations people of other cultures seldom are appointed to leadership positions. Although quotas are not the issue, when a majority of the congregation consists of a minority ethnic group there will be quality leadership material within the group. Those leaders should be discovered, discipled, and dispatched to minister redemptively within the local church. Their calling and gifts cry out to be released in a public setting. They need to be recognized in spite of outward differences of cultural expression.

If a congregation is racially integrated, what would be some practical reasons and some biblical reasons to integrate your leadership?

How do you think a multiracial congregation could assess the leadership needs of its different ethnic components?

How do you think a multiracial congregation could assess the leadership gifts and abilities of men and women in minority ethnic or cultural groups so they aren't overlooked?

THE IMPORTANCE OF PATIENCE AND LOVE

Jesus exhorts us to count the cost before we begin any endeavor (Luke 14:28). There is a definite cost to the development of multiethnic ministry. A large number of people who simply could not adjust to the changes in our congregation left the church. Some of those brothers and sisters were very close to my wife and me. I remember the Sunday that one of our church council members came to me asking, "Just who are we trying to get into this church anyway?"

I responded, "People who are hungry and who know they need the Lord."

On the other hand, some of our black brethren have suffered criticism and racial slurs from their own people because they have chosen to attend a church pastored by a white man. We must realize that deep prejudices have been ingrained in people from childhood. Once we have a clear perception of this matter, we are enabled to respond in love, instead of reacting in anger.

If people from other racial groups started attending your church, what various reactions would you expect?

How would you recommend that your church leadership prepare the congregation if it were going to become more multiracial?

What do you think your church policy should be toward members who object to a multiracial church?

How can a church show compassion to those troubled by fellowshiping and worshiping with believers from other races and cultures without compromising the unifying nature of the gospel?

How do you think Christians from the majority ethnic group in a church should react to the initial suspicions of minority believers who expect to be patronized, manipulated, or ignored?

What do you think are the greatest prices a congregation will pay to become multiracial?

What do you think would be the greatest benefits of becoming a multiracial church?

- For the church

- For the community

1. Tom Morganthau, "Beyond Black and White," *Newsweek* (May 18, 1992), 28.

2. *Spirit-Filled Life® Bible* (Nashville: Thomas Nelson Publishers, 1991), 1645, "Word Wealth: Acts 10:34, partiality."

3. Ibid., 1628, "Word Wealth: Acts 2:42, fellowship."

Lesson 7/ The Necessity of Spiritual Warfare

Greg Howse

Like many pastors I caught a vision for spiritual warfare at the end of the 1980s under the influence of godly men such as C. Peter Wagner and Larry Lea. I began to lead our congregation at Cornerstone Christian Center into spiritual warfare every Sunday evening. We identified five major enemy strongholds in the Chicago Heights area: 1) sexual perversion, 2) violence and corruption, 3) false religions, 4) racism, and 5) pride and rebellion. We have targeted these powers with prayer every week for several years now.

Chicago Heights, Illinois, was the home base of Al Capone's organized crime activities in Chicago. The evil powers we come against in prayer gained their footing in the area during Capone's time. Prostitution, brutality, and political corruption automatically accompanied their Mafia activities. As recently as 1982, right after my family moved to the area, a Mafia leader was assassinated on a nearby golf course.

Pride and rebellion, the major elements of the devil's nature, are the foundation of all these things. When he is allowed to have his way in a community for years at a time, his nature and base characteristics are going to greatly influence people's lives.

IDOLATRY AND INJUSTICE

We need to become more skillful in combating the spiritual forces who are planning and working to destroy our communities through control of proud and rebellious human actions. The New Testament makes it very clear that Christians face principalities and powers, rulers of darkness, and spiritual wickedness in high places (Eph. 6:12). We can march, make speeches, legislate social reforms, and go through religious gymnastics, but none of it will make a long-lasting difference in racial hatred and division until the unseen powers in the spiritual atmosphere of America are engaged in spiritual warfare.

Al Capone didn't operate out of your town. But Satan has had his agents there through the years. What deeply-rooted sins in your community's past and present suggest a pattern of demonic influence that your church and others need to oppose in order to minister effectively there?

What do you think would be some effective ways to mobilize an organized prayer assault against the strongholds of wickedness in your community?

In his book, *Healing America's Wounds,* John Dawson says that demonic influence finds opportunistic access into a city, state, or nation in two basic ways: idolatry and injustice. Dawson identifies America's characteristic idol as Mammon. The power of Mammon is commonly manifested in our land through greed and financial manipulation. Concerning injustice, Dawson says that demonic entrance is found when people wound each other through selfish actions. Rejection, denial, anger, and shame are wounds of injustice marking millions of people in the United States.[1]

How do you think the greedy idol Mammon exerts harmful influence on your community?

How do you think the greedy idol Mammon exerts evil influence even in your church?

What do you think are the greatest injustices people tend to face in your area? How do you think your church should respond to them?

 KINGDOM EXTRA

As Jesus was tempted by the devil in the wilderness, He knew He was there to regain and ultimately win this world's kingdoms and glory, but He would do so only on His Father's terms. The present world systems are largely based on the limited but powerful and destructive rule of the one Jesus called "the ruler of this world" (John 12:31; 16:30). We are wise not to attribute to God anything of the disorder of our confused, sin-riddled, diseased, tragedy-ridden, and torment-ed planet. "This present evil age" (Gal. 1:4) "lies under the sway of the wicked one" (1 John 5:19).[2]

At a pastors' conference in 1995 at The Church On The Way in Van Nuys, California, C. Peter Wagner said that racism is the greatest sin in American culture today. He traced the sin down to the roots of a slave trade that made many rich and an unjust policy toward Native Americans to seize land and natural resources. Wagner's prayer organization targets 126 places where whites massacred Indian women and children as sites where repentance and atonement for these injustices need to occur.[3]

As far as you know, how was your local history affected by slavery?

As far as you know, how was your local history shaped by conflicts with Native Americans?

How do you think the spiritual atmosphere of your community is affected by its history touching slavery and treatment of Native Americans?

DELIVERANCE FROM SPIRITUAL OPPRESSION

In 1995 Cornerstone Christian Center applied for a "special use permit" to use a vacant department store for our ministries. This brought the church leadership into direct negotiations with local government. There were two black and one Hispanic aldermen on the city council by that time. Even though there was a new administration in Chicago Heights, some of the old political tricks continued. The other three aldermen were part of the old regime. They didn't want to see any commercial property outside the control of their cronies.

God used this political process involving a vacant building to stimulate our fight against principalities and powers in heavenly places. The intensity of our prayer ministry went up several notches. We came to realize that God does not care much about that building, but He does care a great deal about the city in which we worship.

We can get a good understanding of the relationship between the kingdom of God and the kingdom of evil by looking at what happened to the children of Israel in the land of Egypt. The Pharaoh of Egypt acted as the instrument of Satan as he attempted to control and enslave God's people. He also reflected the heart of the devil as he feared the potential of God's people to overthrow him (Ex. 1: 9, 10).

Christians are not to be ignorant of the devil's schemes to frustrate the Lord's work in their midst (2 Cor. 2:11). What do you think are some of Satan's main devices to interfere with the success of God's work in your church?

What does the devil have to fear from your church? What are some of its greatest assets for successful outreach into your community?

What do you think is the most positive sign of spiritual victory in the life of your church during the past year? How do you think the devil will try to interfere and turn this into a defeat?

Bible references such as Revelation 12:7–12 (Michael fighting the dragon) and Daniel 10:10–21 (the Prince of Persia and the Prince of Greece hindering Gabriel) reveal an unseen struggle going on in the spiritual realm. The church needs to join with the angelic hosts to bind on earth what has already been bound in the heavens (Matthew 16:13–19). We must discover and apply the true authority of the greater One within us (1 John 4:4), the Spirit of Jesus who came into the world to destroy the works of the devil (1 John 3:8).

 WORD WEALTH

"Proclaim liberty throughout all the land," words from Leviticus 25:10, are inscribed on the Liberty Bell in Philadelphia. The Hebrew word for liberty also is the name for the swallow, a bird swift in flight. In Leviticus 25:10, "liberty" is a technical term for the release of slaves every 50 years in the Year of Jubilee. The Lord Jesus in His first sermon quoted Isaiah 61:1, which states that the Messiah's anointing and divine commission enable Him to "proclaim liberty to the captives" (Luke 4:17–19).[4]

When you pray for worldwide or national concerns, in what ways do you think you should pray that Satan will be bound and prevented from pursuing his agenda?

When you pray for your community, how do you want God to bind Satan and frustrate his plans?

When you consider praying for reconciliation within the church between Christians of different races, how do you think you should pray that God bind the devil?

Pharaoh was afraid of a nation of shepherds (Ex. 1:9) who were totally powerless apart from God. So Pharaoh tried to "deal shrewdly" with Israel so they would never realize he feared their God (v. 10). The devil also plays tricks on the people of God to keep them from recognizing the truth of their power (Eph. 6:11). A lack of knowledge can destroy us (Hos. 4:6) and hold us in captivity (Is. 5:13).

What biblical truths do you think need to be emphasized more in preaching and teaching so believers will be better prepared for spiritual warfare?

The devil uses his finite power to coerce the people of the world to fear him. God will not use His infinite power in the same way. He does not compel belief because the "fear of God" is based on adoration rather than terror. In your opinion, what are the dangers of being fascinated with learning about the devil rather than focusing on God?

How does the devil weaken the strength of the church at war by fostering division between the races?

The foundation of Pharaoh's concern was that Israel would depart from the land of Egypt (Ex. 1:10). He didn't want to lose a source of slave labor. Today the devil doesn't want the church to discover the truth about its authority in Christ. He wants to keep us weakened and defeated by demonically generated oppression around us.

What is supposed to be the greatest difficulty in reaching your community for Christ? How can the devil use this to keep your church from thinking it can be effective in outreach?

What do you think is the greatest single barrier to unity and cooperation between Christians of different races in your community? How can the devil use this to keep your church from thinking it can be effective in racial reconciliation?

The first step for Israel in escaping Egyptian bondage was discovering the power of calling on the name of the Lord (Ex. 2:23, 24; 3:7, 8). In practical terms, what do you think "calling on the name of the Lord" would mean in the spiritual war against interracial suspicion and hatred?

VICTORY OVER SPIRITUAL OPPRESSION

Racism has been entrenched in Chicago Heights. Until recent years, African-Americans were bottled up in one section of town. They were the constant victims of police and political abuse. My secretary's uncle was prominent in the black community of the Heights. In the early 1980s, he implemented positive policies that promoted housing and curtailed drug traffic. The Mafia tried to scare him off. Finally they kidnapped him and pumped him full of mind-altering drugs which left him in a vegetative state the rest of his life.

In the early 1990s, the FBI launched a sharp crackdown on organized crime in the Heights. Several local mayors and their buddies went to prison. Major prostitution rings virtually shut down. Political kickbacks and payoffs slowed to a trickle. The house that my family lives in was built by a Chicago Heights police officer who was selling drugs to the black community. That officer is now in prison. Our congregation emerged as another example in the Chicago area of cross-cultural ministry where blacks, whites, and Hispanics worship and serve together. I believe that the participation of our church and others in spiritual warfare was a major factor in the changes that are going on.

After Israel left Egypt and wandered in the wilderness, the people of God approached the Promised Land. Before entering Canaan, God's people prepared for conquest by battling two Amorite kings on the east side of the Jordan River (Deut. 2:24—3:11). The spiritual battle we are in today is very similar to the battle between Israel and the Amorites. The people of God battle the powers of the world in preparation for entering the kingdom of God.

In Deuteronomy 2:31 God says, "See, I have begun to give Sihon and his land over to you. Begin to possess it." The promises of God are not meant to exclude our efforts. When God initiates any action against our enemies in answer to our prayers, He expects us to participate in the battle through the power of His Spirit and the authority of His name.

What part do you think God expects your church to play in His plan to evangelize your community?

What part do you think God expects your church to play in healing racial tensions in your community?

Three key terms for our participation in spiritual warfare occur in Deuteronomy 2:24: cross over, engage in battle, and possess. To "cross over" is a term used for any transition. There is a transition between ignorance about what is happening in the spiritual realm, becoming knowledgeable about it, and actually getting involved in spiritual warfare. How would God have you "cross over" into a more active role in battling racial bias in your community or church?

To "engage in battle" is a phrase that means to do everything you can to defeat the enemy. In Israel's situation with the Amorites they put their lives in jeopardy before God acted on their behalf. How would God have you "engage in battle" for unity and cooperation among racial and cultural groups?

The term "possess" describes the action of occupying a land by driving out the previous tenants. What attitudes and actions need to become the possession of your church in order to conquer racial hatred in your community?

 KINGDOM EXTRA

The kingdom of God makes its penetration into the world by a kind of violent spiritual conflict and warfare in opposition to the human status quo. The resulting upheaval caused by the kingdom of God is not a result of political provocation or armed advance. It is the result of God's order shaking relationships, households, cities, and nations by the entry of the Holy Spirit's power working in people.[5]

Read Deuteronomy 6:17–19. What are some of the "right" things and "good" things we need to do in the spiritual warfare against racial hatred?

The goal of the physical warfare carried out by the children of Israel was a homeland characterized by pleasant cities and fertile fields that promised a comfortable life. What do you think will be the rewards from God's hand of battling successfully against racial hatred in our communities and our churches?

1. John Dawson, *Healing America's Wounds* (Ventura, CA: Regal Books, 1994), 53–59.

2. *Spirit-Filled Life® Bible* (Nashville: Thomas Nelson Publishers, 1991), 1517, "Kingdom Dynamics: Luke 4:14-32, Earth's Evil 'Ruler.'"

3. C. Peter Wagner, "My Father's House and I Have Sinned," *The Church on the Way Pastors' Seminar,* Tape M2508 (Van Nuys, CA: Sound Word Tape Ministry).

4. *Spirit-Filled Life® Bible,* 181, "Word Wealth: Lev. 25:10, liberty."

5. Ibid., 1424, "Kingdom Dynamics: Matt. 11:12, Taking It by Force."

Part III
"Just Do It!"

In case you are thinking of athletic shoes right about now, it's high time for the church of Jesus Christ to exercise its spiritual muscles in the cause of racial reconciliation. Hearing the truth without doing something about it is frowned upon in the Scripture, so the last part of this study guide focuses on what to do about the truth you've interacted with in the first two sections.

As you make action plans,* be sure you aren't running off in your own strength. That's the wrong gear. "Shod your feet with the preparation of the gospel of peace" (Eph. 6:15) and go do it!

*The topics covered in lessons 8 through 11 correspond with principles 1 through 4 and 6 in *Breaking Down Walls: A Model for Reconciliation in an Age of Racial Strife* (Chicago: Moody Press, 1993), by pastors Raleigh Washington and Glen Kehrein. For more insight into these ideas, Greg Howse and Michael Posey recommend *Breaking Down Walls* to everyone using this study guide.

Lesson 8/"Won't You Be My Neighbor?"

Michael Posey

The atmosphere was tense as I walked a corridor of the data processing facility to my cubicle. It was the day after the jury returned the "not guilty" verdict in the trial of the Los Angeles policemen charged with brutally beating Rodney King. The night before I had sat glued to my television watching parts of Los Angeles go up in smoke. Now in the Sears corporate data-processing center, racial lines were drawn.

Blacks stood in small groups talking about the previous day's events. Some were visibly angry. Most whites silently worked at their desks. The day before these groups had talked eagerly, but not now. The tension was thick enough to cut. As I looked at how this issue was dividing our office I wondered how the members of Cornerstone Christian Center would respond. Over the previous two years our church had shifted from being almost exclusively white to a racially mixed congregation.

It didn't take long for my answer to come. A black member of our church came into my cubicle. He started talking about the verdict. "I'm mad, and I can't handle this anymore." The next words out of his mouth shocked me. "I'm leaving the church. I can't worship with white people or sit under a white pastor any longer."

I tried explaining that we could not judge an entire race by the actions of a few. I asked, "What about the people you've developed relationships with, doesn't that count for anything?"

"I'm leaving, white people cannot be trusted." He never returned to the church.

How could this event affect my friend in such a way? Probably because one of the most important elements of racial reconciliation was missing. Although this man attended a racially-mixed congregation and had his wedding performed by the white pastor, he never committed himself to a relationship with anyone of a different race. So when trouble came he did not maintain any of the cross-cultural relationships he was involved in.

JESUS IS INTO RELATIONSHIPS

Most Christians would agree that development of cross-cultural relationships is important for growth and unity in the church. The reality is that there are many pressures to terminate or neglect friendships with people of different races. Jesus foresaw that with the addition of people to the church, there would be an increase in the diversity of backgrounds, temperaments, and expressions of worship. Not surprisingly He stressed the importance of unity.

Read John 17:20–23 and meditate on it. What are the main ideas Jesus stressed about Christian unity?

What implications does this prayer have for the commitment of Christians of different races to one another?

What would you like to see your church do to show its commitment to glorifying the Lord through Christian unity of different races and cultural groups?

KINGDOM EXTRA

When two people marry, God stands as a witness to the marriage, sealing it with the strongest possible word: *covenant.* "Covenant" speaks of faithfulness and enduring commitment. It stands like a divine sentinel over marriage, for blessing or for judgment. Yet where husband and wife live according to their marriage vows, all the power of a covenant-keeping God stands behind them and their marriage.[1]

You can illustrate any successful covenant by comparing it to marriage. Interracial friendships need the kind of committed covenantal character that causes a marriage to survive its ups and downs. Consider the following four elements of a covenant.[2]

1. *Identification By Name.* In my relationship with Greg Howse there is almost nothing he could do to change my commitment to him, because I know Greg Howse. Our names represent to one another our character and our loyalty.

Reflect on the strongest friendships you have had. What kinds of experiences and conversations would you need to have with a person of another race to know that person by name like these other friends?

2. *Rehearsing The History of the Relationship.* Greg and I went through the transformation of Cornerstone Christian Center from a mostly white congregation to the multiethnic fellowship it is today. Together we prayed, talked, made mistakes, put them right, suffered hurt and misunderstanding, experienced great triumphs, saw friends leave, and made new ones. Occa-

sionally we have to sit down and remember our journey. It's a way to say, "As I have been to you, I will be to you."

With what friend do you talk about the past and the experiences you have shared together? What does that sharing add to your friendship?

What kinds of experiences would you need to go through with a friend from another race before you could really benefit from talking about your shared history?

3. *Promise Making.* In cross-cultural relationships both parties must agree ahead of time to confront every issue that would seek to destroy it. No one can control outside forces that could disturb the relationship—such as racially divisive current events or angry relatives—but the promises you make create a hedge to keep the relationship more secure.

What kinds of troublesome issues do you think inter-racial friends should anticipate needing to face sooner or later?

What guidelines for dealing with divisive problems do you think interracial friends should agree to follow?

4. *Accepting Consequences.* Covenant relationships are meant to be a source of emotional, mental, and spiritual fulfillment, but they can also create indescribable agonies. This is certainly true of cross-cultural relationships. Greg and I both have experienced rejection from people of our individual ethnic background.

What unpleasant consequences should you expect if God directs you to develop and maintain interracial friendships?

What blessings can you expect as the result of obeying God's leading into interracial friendships?

Why do you think God allows so many unpleasant consequences to accompany interracial friendships?

 FAITH ALIVE

Identify a person of a different ethnic background with whom you would like to enter a covenant of friendship.

How would you like to spend time with that person in order to create a special relationship? Circle the letters of all of the options that appeal to you. Add your own.

a. Share breakfast or lunch once a week.
b. Regular exercise or athletics together.
c. Share a hobby.
d. Bible study and prayer.
e. Shop together.
f. Yard work or home repairs.
g. Regular family evenings together.
h. Go to movies or other recreational events.
i. Other.
j. Other.
k. Other.

If you already have a covenant friendship with someone of a different race, how could you strengthen it?

Who Is My Neighbor?

A neighbor is someone who lives close by. When we apply this literal sense to our neighbors in all of mankind, we might conclude that our universal neighbors are those who are "close to us," in the sense of similar to us. Jesus would have none of that kind of reasoning. He told the parable of the good Samaritan to shock everyone who hears it, because that parable identifies our neighbor as anyone in need. A good neighbor is someone who inconveniences herself or risks his reputation for someone in trouble. Jesus' model neighbor—the Samaritan— helped a Jew, a man he was expected to hate.

 KINGDOM EXTRA

The Abrahamic Covenant (Gen. 12:1–3) established moral obligations among the Israelites. They were command- ed to show concern for their neighbors. The ninth and tenth commandments (Ex. 20:16–17; Deut. 5:20–21) prohibited the defaming or slandering of a neighbor and condemned the envying of neighbor's wife, servant, livestock, or other pos- sessions. A person was not to cheat or rob from his neighbor (Lev. 19:13). Despising one's neighbor was sin (Prov. 14:21), as was leading him morally astray (Prov. 16:29–30) or deceiv- ing him, then saying, " I was only joking" (Prov. 26:19) A per- son was not even permitted to think evil of his neighbor (Zech. 8:17).[3]

If your neighbor is anyone who needs you, what individu- als and groups in your community have the greatest claims on you as their neighbor? Why?

Jesus told the story of the good Samaritan to a lawyer who tried to limit the group that he had to treat as his neigh- bor (Luke 10:29). We do that too. For instance, some say that Israel was forbidden to marry or form close alliances outside their race, so we shouldn't either. What reasons have you heard for limiting contacts with people of other races?

How does the parable of the good Samaritan (Luke 10:30–37) answer the reasons you recorded in the previous question?

The parable of the good Samaritan implies that racial prejudice could cut us off from receiving help—perhaps vital help—from people of other races. In what ways do you think our lives are made poorer when we isolate ourselves from other races?

 WORD WEALTH

Had compassion translates a Greek verb derived from the noun for viscera or internal organs. The Greeks regarded the bowels as the place where strong and powerful emotions originated. Similarly the Hebrews regarded the viscera as the source of tender mercies and feelings of affection, compassion, sympathy, and pity. Such deep-seated compassion was the direct motive for at least five of Jesus' miracles.[4]

When have you seen a person treated unjustly because of his or her race? How did you respond inwardly and outwardly to that incident? How do you think you should have responded?

Why do you think Jesus included racial and cultural diversity in His parable when answering the question, "Who is my neighbor?" (Luke 10:30–33)

FAITH ALIVE

Imagine you were going to rewrite the parable of the good Samaritan in terms of the racial dynamics of your community or neighborhood. Who would be the majority race?

The road to Jericho was a high-crime area. What would be a corresponding nearby dangerous place?

Who would be a likely crime victim there?

What kind of crime would lead to assault and injury in your high-crime area?

Who would be the reputable but busy folks who could not get involved with the injured person?

Who would be the least likely minority-race hero to intervene and sacrifice himself or herself for the victim?

On a blank page at the end of this book, paraphrase the parable of the good Samaritan using your setting and characters.

It's unlikely that you would frequent the place you described in your version of the parable. How can you be involved in being a neighbor to the truly needy in your community?

How do you think your church could be a better neighbor to the truly needy in your community?

In the parable of the good Samaritan, Jesus makes it clear that love should not be limited by its object. Love is demonstrated in action, and love may be costly. Jesus challenged the lawyer not to talk the talk of being a Christian without walking the walk when he said, "Go and do likewise."

 KINGDOM EXTRA

There was distinct racial strain between Jews and Samaritans (John 4:29). They did not frequently interact with one another; and in some cases, outright hostility and hatred existed. But Jesus, early in His ministry, taught the Samaritans the truth of God. He ministered to "the woman of Samaria" and to the people of Samaria (John 4:4–42).

Here in this parable the source of assistance was not a kinsman or fellow citizen of Israel but a despised Samaritan. We are reminded that one of the great tragedies of prejudice is that it may separate one from a potential source of assistance. The compassion of the Samaritan was all the more commendable in that the person he assisted probably would not have even spoken to him under normal circumstances. Christ has come to break down such division.[5]

FAITH ALIVE

What specific category of people do you have a problem relating to? As someone from Asian ancestry, perhaps it is African-Americans who seem to you to be lazy and violent. As a black female, maybe it's blond-haired white women married to black men. For blue-collar white males, it could be any middle class minorities that got jobs through affirmative action.

How does God expect you to begin relating to people like this as your neighbor?

Ask the Holy Spirit to reveal to you other people you do not want to be your neighbor. Determine to initiate a relationship within that group. If the first person doesn't respond favorably, don't give up. Try again.

1. *Spirit-Filled Life® Bible* (Nashville: Thomas Nelson Publishers, 1991), 1385, "Kingdom Dynamics: Mal. 2:13, 14, 16, God Backs Up the Covenant of Marriage."

2. Daniel A. Brown, *Unlock the Power of Family* (Nashville: Sparrow Press, 1994), 57–59.

3. "Neighbor," *Hayford's Bible Handbook* (Nashville: Thomas Nelson Publishers, 1995), 712.

4. *Spirit-Filled Life® Bible,* 1432, "Word Wealth: Matt. 14:14, moved with compassion."

5. Ibid., 1534, "Kingdom Dynamics: Luke 10:33, Help from a Despised Source."

Lesson 9/Do It on Purpose

Michael Posey

There was a family of black children already playing in the hotel swimming pool as Jeff's three children jumped in. Jeff noticed that almost instinctively the black children moved to a different part of the pool, as if to vacate this end for the white children. Jeff smiled to himself. A few weeks ago he wouldn't have paid much attention to this incident but with the teaching from a workshop on racial reconciliation still fresh in his head, he understood the need to be deliberate in order to destroy racial barriers. He called his son and two daughters over and said, "Go make friends with those kids."

Jeff's children looked at him and then eased over and began talking with the other boys and girls and eventually they began playing together. The children playing together created an excellent avenue for Jeff to use to initiate a conversation with their parents. Throughout the remainder of their stay at the hotel both families spent much time together and both families' stays were enhanced by the friendship that developed.

Can you remember seeing or being a participant in an incident similar to the children moving to a different area of the pool? How did you respond? How did you feel?

If you are a parent what do you think your children would do if you asked them to initiate a friendship with children of another race?

Pre-Meditations About Reconciliation

Reconciliation takes place when we understand the need to be deliberate, to plan positive actions that promote reconciliation. We must be willing to take the first step and sometimes the second and third steps as well. There must be a willingness to go out of our way to develop cross-cultural relationships. Usually a risk factor is involved, because you are never sure how someone will respond to your actions.

In John 4, Jesus deliberately set out to encounter someone His culture told Him to avoid—a Samaritan woman. Her gender was wrong. Strike one! Her moral life was worse. Strike two! And her ethnic group was worst of all. Strike three! Get out of here!

Why do you think Jesus decided that He needed to go through Samaria to get to Galilee? (John 4:3, 4)

How was Jesus "being deliberate" when He met the Samaritan woman at the well?

What emotions do you think the woman was experiencing when Jesus, a Jew, asked her for a drink? (John 4:7–9) Explain why you think this was so.

What emotions or thoughts do you tend to have when you have to have close contacts with people of another race? Why?

In John 4:12 the Samaritan woman identified with Jacob as the father of the Samaritans. Why do you think Jesus deliberately choose Jacob's well for this encounter with the Samaritan woman?

 KINGDOM EXTRA

Human value cannot be equated with race, wealth, social standards, or educational level. To regard a race, group, or individual as less important than another is sin in view of the fact that Christ died for all people and for each one in particular. At the foot of the Cross we are equal, both in our worth to God (He sent His Son to die for each of us) and in our need to accept His gift of salvation. Let us learn to respect and honor every person and each people regardless of their station or color. Christ said, "Inasmuch as you did it to one of the least of these My brethren, you did it to Me" (Matt. 25:40).[1]

In John 4:20 the woman tried to pit Samaritans against Jews. How did Jesus handle her challenge? What do you think He wanted to accomplish with His answer?

John 4:23 and 24 outline the kind of agreement that crosses every line of racial and cultural bias. Fill in the blanks based on these two verses.

God is _____.

True worshipers must worship in _____

and_____.

How do these truths challenge the pride and suspicion that form the basis of all racial divisions?

WORD WEALTH

The Greek term for **worship** had the idea in it of bowing down and kissing the ground. From this came the general ideas of prostrating oneself, bowing down, showing reverence, worshiping, and adoring. In the New Testament the word especially denotes homage rendered to God and the ascended Christ. All believers have a one-dimensional worship directed toward the only Lord and Savior. We do not worship angels, saints, shrines, relics, or ethnicity.[2]

WORD WEALTH

The Greek word translated **truth** was a compound made up of a negative prefix and a verb meaning "to be hidden," "to escape notice." "Truth" is the opposite of fictitious, feigned, or false. It denotes veracity, reality, sincerity, accuracy, integrity, truthfulness, dependability, and propriety. As Jesus used it when talking to the Samaritan woman at the well, "truth" meant reality stripped of all the confusing traditions of man-made religion.[3]

FAITH ALIVE

Identify two or three occasions on which you were uncomfortable in the presence of people of another ethnic group. What was it that made you feel disconnected and isolated from them?

1.

2.

3.

After reading how Jesus handled this encounter with the Samaritan woman, how could you have handled these encounters deliberately and constructively?

1.

2.

3.

For a church to become deliberate in promoting racial reconciliation, people must receive a revelation of the value of people they may not previously have valued. How did Jesus reveal to His disciples the value of the Samaritans whom they despised? (John 4:35)

How can you tell when you are treating someone as though they have no value? When did you last do so?

How do you feel about people joining your church who appear to have nothing to offer, but will possibly begin to drain resources?

What was the fruit of Jesus' deliberate outreach to people of a hated ethnic group? (John 4:39–42)

What positive results can you imagine happening in your community if your church reached out to people ordinarily ignored or excluded by social pressures?

COLOR IS EVERYWHERE. SEE IT!

In addition to being deliberate about building interracial friendships, we have to know how to be sensitive to the dynamics between different racial groups. We cannot be color-blind. Many times when talking to people of different ethnic backgrounds I hear the statement, "I don't see color." I understand their heart, but I point out that there are times we need to see color. Almost everyone around us is aware of color. If you are the only Asian in a room full of blacks, believe me you are aware of color. Seeing color does not translate into racism. It simply allows you to be sensitive.

Imagine you have to walk to pick up your car from the shop. The shortest route is a busy street straight through a section of town where there are people of an ethnic background with whom you don't usually associate. There is a jogging path that is longer, because it goes around this section of town. Some of your friends have advised you to go the longer way. Which path would you choose? Why?

Let's look at how Jesus responded when this situation presented itself. Read John 4:9–26. What parts of the story show that Jesus did not ignore that the woman was a Samaritan?

How did Jesus disagree with Samaritan traditions without demeaning the woman's ethnic background or flaunting His own? (John 4:21–24)

Read John 4:27–42. Both Jesus and His disciples were conscious of the ethnic lines between them and the Samaritans. How did the disciples' ethnic consciousness make them insensitive to the spiritual needs of the Samaritans?

How did Jesus' ethnic consciousness make Him more sensitive to the spiritual needs of the Samaritans?

 KINGDOM EXTRA

To love the unlovable is to separate ourselves from the world's self-serving kind of love—to share Christ's love with people who have no apparent ability to return anything at all. Jesus calls us to love as He did—to love those who finish last, those who are ugly, those who are poor, or who are powerless to help us. This response is only possible by a supernatural transformation that begets in us a different order of response than is usual to mankind. When we become better at viewing people through the eyes of God, we find that many people we thought were unlovable are actually very lovely. It was just our biased ways of seeing that needed to change.[4]

In contemporary life, how can our color consciousness act either to dull or sharpen our sensitivities to the emotional and spiritual needs of people of other races with whom we come in contact?

- Dull

- Sharpen

 FAITH ALIVE

A young interracial couple renewed their commitments to Christ and became very involved in the ministries of a predominantly white congregation in a midwestern city. They became involved in discipleship and outreach ministries of the church. When they wanted to team teach a children's Sunday school class, some white parents objected to an interracial couple as a model for their children. The church did not let them teach together. What messages did this church action send?

• To the interracial couple

• To the parents who objected

• To the Lord Jesus

What action do you think the church leadership should have taken in this situation?[5]

What, if anything, would you tell the interracial couple?

What, if anything, would you tell the objecting parents?

TAKE THE PLUNGE

Like Jeff's children at the swimming pool, you'll never start having an impact on the ethnic and cultural character of your church until you go over and meet the people of another race who are close by. Talk with your pastor or a mature Christian friend about what you sense God is leading you to do. Bathe your efforts in prayer. Then go make some new friends.

Where and when do you have contact with people of other races or cultures?

With whom among these existing contacts could you build a friendship? What would be the most natural way to initiate social contacts?

How could you reach out beyond your normal social circles to meet people of another race or culture whom you ordinarily would never meet?

What interests, hobbies, community involvements, or other parts of your life could serve as points of contact with people of other races or cultures outside your normal circle?

KINGDOM EXTRA

In Leviticus 19:34, God reminds His people that they, who once were foreigners in the land of Egypt, should above all others remember how it feels to be treated as outsiders. Lesson 1: Remember how rejection feels, and never manifest it. His further instructions on the treatment of strangers are opposite to normal, worldly standards. The Lord says that when strangers come into our homes, they are to be treated as "one born among you," that is, as blood relatives! Lesson 2: All humanity is one family. Treat others that way.[6]

In the space below, write out an action plan you would like to implement in order to build a deliberate friendship that is sensitive to color and all other differences between you and a person of another race or culture.

1. *Spirit-Filled Life® Bible* (Nashville: Thomas Nelson Publishers, 1991), 1897, "Kingdom Dynamics: James 2:1-9, Respect of Persons."

2. Ibid., 1967, "Word Wealth: Rev. 4:10, worship."

3. Ibid., 1580, "Word Wealth: John 4:24, truth."

4. Ibid., 1522, "Kingdom Dynamics: Luke 6:31-35, God's Love Loves the Unlovable."

5. The church leadership could have issued a policy statement affirming the commitment of the church to people of all ethnic groups as worshipers and as leaders whenever qualified. Leaders should meet with each offended parent in an effort to make peace and achieve reconciliation.

6. *Spirit-Filled Life® Bible*, 172-173, "Kingdom Dynamics: Lev. 19:34, Unselfish Christian Love Toward Strangers."

Lesson 10/Do It with a Tender Heart

Michael Posey

It was hard to leave our old church. Cathy and I got married there. Our friends and memories were there. For the first time in six years we didn't know where we were going to worship next Sunday. Steve, a black brother in the Lord, invited me to the church that sponsored his kids' school. So on Sunday my family met at Steve's house and followed him to Cornerstone Christian Center.

I wasn't prepared for what I saw. The congregation was 95% white. "No big deal," I said inside. "I'll sit through this one service, pack up my family, and never come back." I knew God wasn't leading us to a white church.

But a strange thing happened. Everybody else in my family loved it. My kids were so excited about children's church that they asked to go back. For three weeks we were at this church, and each week the pastor preached about my life. I attended this white church, I was down at the altar crying!

I had a big problem. Cathy suggested I talk to the pastor. He and his wife seemed friendly. I thought they actually wanted us there. So I took a chance and set up a meeting. If this was where God wanted us, I didn't want to be a hindrance.

I walked into Greg's office and talked about things I had never shared with another man. Finally I told him I wasn't comfortable around white people. I didn't trust them. I let them intimidate me. What could I do? I emptied my heart to this white guy and sat there wondering what he would say. Could he understand how difficult it was for me to say these things? Could I trust him?

Greg responded with understanding, honesty, and compassion. He acknowledged that he didn't have answers for everything I was dealing with, but could understand why. This was the first of many conversations we had as we learned more about each other, ourselves, and other races. In the months to follow the truth challenged our assumptions. Our perceptions changed as we learned to view the world through someone else's eyes. This process involved two key ingredients: sincerity and sensitivity.

TOLERATION AIN'T RECONCILIATION

Raleigh Washington and Glen Kehrein are another interracial ministry team in the Chicago area. They define sincerity as "the willingness to be vulnerable, including the self-disclosure of feelings, attitudes, differences, and perceptions, with the goal of resolution and building trust."[1]

Jesus modeled this kind of sincerity when He called His disciples friends (John 15:14).

WORD WEALTH

Friends is one of the beautiful words of the Bible. It's the "phil-" part of philanthropy, philosophy, and Philadelphia. An adjective used as a noun, *philos* denotes a loved one or an affectionate friend. This kind of friendship is based on natural and mutual attraction between the friends. *Philos* thus has congeniality about it.[2]

What is the difference between building real friendships with people and building relationships that are utilitarian? (John 15:15)

By what standard are we to gauge our love for our friends? (John 15:12)

What is the greatest display of love for our friends? How did Jesus demonstrate His love for His? (John 15:13)

Based on Jesus' idea of Christian friendship, what are some costs you can foresee paying to establish and maintain a friendship with someone of another race or culture?

Jesus started out as the master of a group of disciples and ended up as their sincere friend (John 15:15). The hallmark of that sincerity was transparency. Jesus' desire for this level of friendship was not reactive but proactive. He initiated it.

Jesus found that sincere friendships with His disciples left Him vulnerable to betrayal. When Judas betrayed Jesus with a kiss (Matt. 26:49), he used the most intimate expression of friendship to point Jesus out to the posse charged with bringing Him in.

Even while Judas betrayed Him, Jesus called him "friend" (Matt. 26:50). Why do you think He did so?

 KINGDOM EXTRA

Being vulnerable as a leader means to stand totally open as a human being, hiding nothing and refusing to defend oneself. Few things elicit more of a response from people than to sense they are dealing with someone who feels their pain and understands their need, which they only discover if the leader is vulnerable enough to disclose as much. When Jesus refused to defend Himself the night of His arrest, Peter's protective action severed the ear of the high priest's bodyguard. Immediately, Jesus reached out to heal His enemy, making Himself vulnerable to a return sword thrust, since His reaching for the man's head easily could have been interpreted as another hostile move. Vulnerability may expose to misunderstanding, but it will also bring healing.[3]

Not only did Jesus refuse to defend himself when betrayed, but He assisted the man wounded by one of His friends (Luke 22:51). In the ministry of reconciliation we must watch for defensiveness. In what areas of your life do you tend to be defensive?

How might this defensiveness be detrimental in the developing and maintaining of sincere cross-cultural relationships?

Identify a time you attempted to be transparent in a cross-cultural relationship. What was the outcome?

Why do you think this attempt at sincere transparency succeeded or failed?

It's hard to share your life—"background, home life, strengths and weaknesses, relationship struggles, thoughts and attitudes, dreams and goals, reactions and feelings"[4] with someone from another race. Paul demonstrated this type of openness with the Thessalonian Christians, who remained his special friends throughout his life.

What evidences of sincerity, openness, and vulnerability do you find in Paul's description of his relationship with the Thessalonians? (1 Thess. 2:1–12)

What do you think motivates a leader to care for people as Paul did in 1 Thessalonians 2:8?

If you enter a cross-cultural relationship, what would it mean for you to impart your life to that one?

  FAITH ALIVE

Rod Cooper, national director of education for Promise Keepers, lists five levels of relationships.
- The first level is talking about the weather, sports or other inconsequential matters.
- The second level is to offer an opinion about the weather or sports.
- The third level is the expression of a belief.
- The fourth is when others share their dreams, fears, and emotions with me.
- The fifth is when I share my dreams, fears, and emotions with others.[5]

Without naming names, give an example of each level of relationship from your circle of friends.

1.

2.

3.

4.

5.

Many people with cross-cultural relationships never get past the third level. Some function in level four but never move to level five. They think they have intimate relationships but they need to share their lives as well.

Who is your best friend of another race?

At what level is your relationship with that friend operating?

What can you do to move that relationship to level five?

SAYING WHAT POLITE PEOPLE NEVER SAY

The response to the verdict rendered in the 1995 O.J. Simpson trial illuminated the conflicting views on the status of race relations in America. All across the land television cameras were positioned to capture the response of Americans as the verdict was read. The cameras showed jubilant blacks celebrating the "not guilty" verdict while whites sat stunned in disbelief.

In the days to follow this was "the topic" on every talk radio station in Chicago and, I suspect, the nation. There was one question in particular that caught my interest while driving, "If you are white, are you able to discuss the verdict with a black friend?" (The reverse question was posed to blacks.) Many people responded with a "no."

There were such strong conflicting emotions attached to the O.J. decision that many people did not feel comfortable discussing it with someone of another race. So blacks talked to blacks about whites, and whites talked to whites about blacks. The O.J. trial merely illustrated the danger of people of one ethnic group talking about another ethnic group. Usually this just reinforces stereotypes.

The Old Testament law contained a statute against this kind of behavior. What term did the Law attach to those who talk about others instead of to them? (Lev. 19:16)

What kinds of things motivate us to speak ill of people of other races? (Lev. 19:17; Prov. 18:8)

If you've been accustomed to thinking and speaking badly of another ethnic group, how do you think you can change that pattern?

It's touchy, but it is necessary in cross-cultural relationships to go to your brother and talk things out openly and honestly. How do you think truth and love need to cooperate in order to produce sincere Christian friendships across racial lines? (Eph. 4:15)

What happens to sincere communication in an interracial friendship when either truth or love is missing?
- Truth without love

- Love without truth

Ephesians 4:25–32 traces a progression of steps in building a sincere relationship. Identify the step to a strong relationship in each of the following verses and apply it to establishing a sincere interracial friendship.
1. (Eph. 4:25)

2. (Eph. 4:26, 27)

3. (Eph. 4:29)

4. (Eph. 4:30, 31)

5. (Eph. 4:32)

Please, Listen with Your Heart

The second ingredient in the relationship Greg Howse and I have built is sensitivity. Washington and Kehrein describe sensitivity as "the intentional acquisition of knowledge in order to relate empathetically to a person of a different race and culture."[6]

Communication is essential in the ministry of racial reconciliation. But because we come from diverse backgrounds and communities, we sometimes don't know how to start. For example, I have heard many whites admit the fear of referring to someone in the black community with the wrong terminology. There was a time when "Negro" or "Colored" was proper, then the social term changed to "Black," and more recently "African-American" is being used. To some this may not seem like a big issue, but I have seen the issue of correct terminology become an obstacle in healing the rift between the races. Reconciliation can be difficult if we are only sensitive to words and not to hearts. I call sensitivity "listening with your heart."

Sensitivity means being aware of uncomfortable situations for your brother of a different race. Greg was asked to perform a funeral for a relative of a black couple in our church. This was the first black funeral at which Greg officiated. Usually Greg and I assist each other with cultural customs in order not to offend anyone because of ignorance. On this occasion I was out of town. Greg had a relationship with the black pastor of the church where the funeral was being held. This man stayed close by and helped Greg when he ran into any unfamiliar areas. Greg wanted to be sensitive to the people he was ministering to, and this pastor was sensitive to Greg.

The Book of Proverbs contains several sayings about sensitivity in speaking and listening. What do you think Solomon meant when he said that the heart of the wise teaches his mouth? (Prov. 16:23)

Why do you think it's so hard to regain someone's confidence after offending them with racially insensitive remarks or actions? (Prov. 18:19)

 KINGDOM EXTRA

The theme of brotherhood emerges early in Scripture; and from the very beginning, it is clear that God places a high priority on how brothers treat each other. In Genesis 4:1–9 the question of responsibility for one another first emerges. Cain asks, "Am I my brother's keeper?" The word used for "keeper" (Hebrew *shamar*) means "to guard, to protect, to attend, or to regard." Are we responsible? "Absolutely," is God's answer. Not only are we our brother's keeper, we are held accountable for our treatment of and our ways of relating to our brothers (blood and spiritual).

For Cain's sins against his brother, God curses him throughout the Earth, takes away his ability to farm, and sentences him to a life as a fugitive and a vagabond (v.12). This clearly indicates that unbrotherliness destines one to fruitlessness and frustration of purpose.[7]

The Lord asked Cain, "Where is Abel your brother?" Cain replied, "Am I my brother's keeper?" (Gen. 4:9). How does God's question challenge you to promote unity between racial and cultural groups in the body of Christ?

122 🐾 Race and Reconciliation

Paul the apostle to the Gentiles truly understood the need for sensitivity. On the positive side, he made a point of adapting his speech and pattern of life to whatever culture he ministered in at the time (1 Cor. 9:19–23). On the negative side, Paul tried to avoid anything that offended those he served (8:13).

How can our insensitivities offend our brothers and sisters in Christ of other races?

When do you think such offenses are our fault and when the fault of the one taking offense?

What are some practical steps you can take to become better informed and more sensitive to other ethnic groups?

In what area of racial relations do you need to work so that you do not give offense and hurt believers of other races?

1. Raleigh Washington and Glen Kehrein, *Breaking Down Walls* (Chicago: Moody Press, 1993), 141.
2. *Spirit-Filled Life® Bible* (Nashville: Thomas Nelson Publishers, 1991), 1595, "Word Wealth: John 11:11, friend."
3. Ibid., 1458-1459, "Kingdom Dynamics: Matt. 26:47-54, Vulnerability."
4. *Breaking Down Walls,* 144.
5. Rod Cooper, "INTO-ME-SEE/Intimacy," *New Man* (March/April 1995), 42.
6. *Breaking Down Walls,* 155.
7. *Spirit-Filled Life® Bible,* 11, "Kingdom Dynamics: Gen. 4:9, Responsibilty for One Another."

Lesson 11/Do It Carrying Your Cross

Greg Howse

In the fall of 1994 I took a team of eight from Cornerstone Christian Center on a short-term missions trip to Croatia. We determined before we went on the journey that we were not going as a bunch of hotshot, know-it-alls, telling everyone how to be Christians the "American way." We intentionally humbled ourselves, first before the Lord, second before one another, and then before the saints we were with in Croatia.

All we wanted to do was give away whatever element of God's grace was at work in us. And each of us wanted to learn as much as possible from our brothers and sisters in the cities of Dubrovnik, Split, and Zagreb. That intentional mind-set gave us a deep sense of love and respect for saints of God we had never met before. They opened their lives to us, responding to our desire to serve them. It was a wonderful experience.

We were Americans—black and white—on a cross-cultural adventure. Every principle of this study applied. What we did we did deliberately, sincerely, and sensitively. Roll all of those factors together and they add up to sacrifice—a very Christlike quality.

Fellow pastors Raleigh Washington and Glen Kehrein define sacrifice as "the willingness to relinquish an established status or position to genuinely adopt a lesser position in order to facilitate a cross-cultural relationship."[1] This kind of sacrifice is absolutely mandatory for success in a cross-cultural relationship.

TAKE THE LOWLY PLACE

The Arthurian legends will never die. Not too long ago a movie titled *First Knight* brought King Arthur, Lancelot,

Guinevere, and Camelot to the big screen once more. At one point in the story King Arthur and his knights gathered at the round table. Arthur explained its shape by saying that in Camelot no knight is better or higher than another, but everyone lives to serve the others. There were no places of honor at the round table; all were seats of service.

Because of the ethnic makeup of our local congregation, I am often involved in situations in which I am the only Caucasian. I try to be intentional about taking the lesser position whenever I can. Sometimes people try to get me to be more assertive, but I resist that because it will not facilitate long-lasting relationships, filled with mutual respect if I'm always throwing my weight around as the white pastor.

Jesus told a story about an oriental wedding feast that went on for a long time. All of the guests jockeyed for positions of visibility and prestige (Luke 14:7–11).

What's the danger of wanting to be important? (Luke 14:8, 9)

What's the advantage of approaching life as the servant of others? (Luke 14:10)

Why should you "sit down in the lowest place" in a cross-cultural relationship?

How can you "sit down in the lowest place" in a cross-cultural relationship?

How will humbling yourself in this way open the way for you to "go up higher?"

 KINGDOM EXTRA

Love is servant-spirited. The worldly-mind will never understand or accept this call. A servant is one who accepts and acknowledges a place beneath those whom he serves, one willing to forsake the systems of social status on our human scale of values. Servants are viewed as performing the unworthy tasks considered beneath those whom they serve. But Jesus says that those who function as His servants—serving the world in His name—will be honored by the heavenly Father. Every true servant will ultimately be honored by the One whom they serve and who has promised them honor for that service![2]

LET HIS MIND BE IN YOU

Philippians 2:5–11 is a call for believers to see Jesus as their example of humility. Jesus did not have to grasp or seize equality with God, because He already was God. Instead, He intentionally gave up His majestic glory to come to earth and take on the identity of humanity. First, He humbled Himself as a man. Next He became a servant. Finally He stooped to the point of death on the cross.

Jesus did all of this for the sake of relationship. His actions redeemed mankind and reconciled them to God. His is the definitive example of sacrifice. Jesus gave up His exalted status in the presence of the Father to adopt a lesser position in order to facilitate the ultimate cross-cultural relationship—heaven to earth.

What would you have to give up in order to pursue friendships with people of other races?

What would your church have to give up in order to develop an interracial ministry in your community?

One of the following two questions doesn't apply directly to your racial status. Perhaps you could ask the opinion of a friend from another ethnic group. If you do, don't be defensive. Listen to learn.

What attitudes do you think a majority-race person has to let go of in order to become a servant of a minority-race person?

What attitudes do you think a minority-race person has to let go of in order to become a servant of a majority-race person?

Sometimes it takes greater humility to accept service from a person of another race than to give it. Why do you think this is so?

SACRIFICE MEANS COUNTING THE COST

When our local congregation began to go through its ethnic and cultural change, a lot of whites left us to go elsewhere. In some cases they left because they did not want their children to grow into the perilous teen years being close to blacks. The thinking goes like this—if you grow up with them, spend friendship time with them, and date them, you have a very good chance of . . . you know.

Are cross-cultural friendships a disadvantage for our children? Well, I suppose you could see a disadvantage in almost any situation. However, I believe that children who grow up with cross-cultural exposure will be better equipped to function successfully in life at the adult level. They are growing up into a cross-cultural world.

There is a definite cost to the development of cross-cultural ministry. My wife and I lost close friends. Black friends have been called "Oreos" and accused of trying to be like "whitey." White friends have been called "nigger lovers." Both have been called "wannabes." Not everyone is willing or ready to pay the cost to win the prize of unity within the body of Christ.

How do you think a person engaged in interracial friendships should respond to rejection by family, friends, and others who are close?

How do you think a person engaged in interracial ministry should deal with the feelings of being a traitor to his or her own people?

What price of rejection do you think you might face if God directed you into a ministry of racial reconciliation?

 KINGDOM EXTRA

Victory comes only through battle, and triumph only follows trial. Only a weak view of the truth of the kingdom of God pretends otherwise. Another weak view surrenders to negative circumstances on the proposition that we are predestined to problems and therefore should merely tolerate them. The Bible teaches that suffering, trial, and all other human difficulty are unavoidable; but God's Word also teaches they may all be overcome. The presence of the King and the power of His kingdom in our lives makes us neither invulnerable nor immune to life's struggles. But they do bring the promise of victory: provision in need, strength for the day, and healing, comfort, and saving help.[3]

UNLEASH THE POWER OF REPENTANCE AND FORGIVENESS

Whenever people try to talk about racial tension, that very conversation creates more racial tension. Some of us, unfortunately, react with rejection, anger, and blame. Sometimes racial biases are so deep-seated that they need to be repented of. Repentance is a deliberate admission that past thinking and reacting were wrong and must be replaced with patterns of thinking and reacting based on God's truth. This repentance opens the way for us to give and receive forgiveness. Forgiveness empowers individuals or groups to release their heavy burdens of guilt and defensiveness.

KINGDOM EXTRA

The first call of the kingdom of God is to repentance. The implications of biblical repentance are threefold: 1) renunciation and reversal, 2) submission and teachability, and 3) continual shapeability. There is no *birth* into the kingdom without hearing the call of salvation, renouncing one's sins, and turning from sin to Christ the Savior.

There is no *growth* in the kingdom without obedience to Jesus' commandments and a childlike responsiveness as a disciple of Jesus, yielding to the teaching of God's Word.

There is no lifelong increase of *fruit* as a citizen of the kingdom without a willingness to accept the Holy Spirit's correction and guidance.[4]

Why do you think majority-race members tend to feel no particular personal guilt for the biases and injustices of society as a whole?

Why do you think minority-race members tend to feel that majority-race members are personally responsible for the biases and injustices of society as a whole?

Of what attitudes or behaviors toward other races do you (majority-race or minority-race member) need to repent?

On the cross Jesus prayed for all who had conspired and participated in His death, "Father, forgive them, for they do not know what they are doing" (Luke 23:34). His sacrifice and willingness to forgive brought us together with God, whom we now call Father. He calls on us to express that same sacrificial and forgiving spirit wherever there is alienation from God and other people.

How do you think Jesus was able to shake off the tendency to blame others, and forgive the ones who were being so cruel to Him?

How can you develop a Christlike attitude of forgiveness in the often hostile arena of racial reconciliation?

C. Peter Wagner is pioneering an area of repentance that some find radical and others find liberating. He calls it "identificational repentance." It follows the example of key Old Testament leaders who led Israel in repentance for the sins of their ancestors in order to prepare for revival.

Describe the "identificational repentance" of each of these leaders for historical sins of Israel.

Moses (Ex. 32:31, 32)

Daniel (Dan. 9:15, 16)

Ezra (Ezra 9:6, 7)

Nehemiah (Neh. 1:6, 7)

Wagner heads a prayer ministry which is sending representatives to various sites in America where atrocities were committed against American Indians. These intercessors are going
to these locations to repent of the sins perpetrated against
innocent Indian women and children. They are doing this
even though they were not directly responsible for such sinful
acts.

Wagner's group is also sending representatives into
Europe to retrace the travels of the Crusaders who brutalized
Jews and Muslims in the name of Christ. These intercessors
will repent of the acts of the Crusaders and acknowledge the
resultant hostility both Jews and Muslims hold against Christians.

What spiritual value can you see in acknowledging the sins
of our ancestors and fellow countrymen?

What are the risks you run if you acknowledge the sins of
your ancestors in the presence of unforgiving members of
other races?

What possibilities for growth of relationships and commitments between Christians of different races are opened up by
admitting the sins of our ancestors?

FAITH ALIVE

There are three steps to spiritual freedom in cross-cultural relationships:

1. Confess faults, errors, and trespasses to God (1 John 1:9) and to one another (James 5:16). What would it be liberating for you to confess to God or to a friend of another race?

2. Submit yourself to God (James 4:6, 7). What element of ethnic pride do you need to submit to God so you can serve Him sacrificially in promoting racial reconciliation?

3. Commit yourself to covenant relationships (1 Sam. 18:3, 4). What sacrificial commitments do you need to make in a cross-cultural friendship that mirrors the godly friendship of David and Jonathan?

1. Raleigh Washington and Glen Kehrein, *Breaking Down Walls* (Chicago: Moody Press, 1993), 185.

2. *Spirit-Filled Life® Bible* (Nashville: Thomas Nelson Publishers, 1991), 1598, "Kingdom Dynamics: John 12:26, Love Is Servant-Spirited."

3. Ibid., 1654, "Kingdom Dynamics: Acts 14:21, 22, Suffering, Tribulation."

4. Ibid., 1407, "Kingdom Dynamics: Matthew 3:1, 2; 4:17, repentance."

Lesson 12/Set the Captives Free

Michael Posey and Greg Howse

As I sat in the cafeteria of the corporation where I worked before entering the ministry, I couldn't help but overhear the two men talking. One fellow in particular wanted me to hear this conversation since I am black. "No, I didn't get the promotion, even though I was the most qualified. They passed all of us over except Bill. Out of the five spots available three blacks and one Hispanic got the other jobs. Man, I'm telling you the average white man doesn't stand a chance in this country with these affirmative action quotas. No matter how hard you work they give the jobs to some minority."

Melissa is a black divorcée with three children. She feels much the same way the white guy does. The father of her children never provides financial support, because he doesn't work. For a long time Melissa worked minimum-wage jobs, but she couldn't make enough to support her family. She tried working and going to night school so she could get a better job. Her kids' grades went down and they starting getting in trouble in school. So Melissa stays home raising her kids and draws public assistance. Melissa voices her feelings of hopelessness and rejection: "I'm a black woman with three children and few skills. The system is set to keep me down."

Maybe neither of these illustrations pertains to you. But perhaps you have been denied a job or home based on your race and you feel powerless. Perhaps you can't seem to get started into the economic life of your community and you feel held down. It appears we are fast becoming a society of victims. If we aren't careful, our every thought and attitude can be shaped by the assumption that life-killing injustices have been perpetrated against us.

Warning that the victim syndrome can be a spiritual problem does not minimize the seriousness of the injustice. It acknowledges the injustice but recognizes the power of God to transform victims rather than leaving them mired in self-pity. Left to itself the victim mentality often aligns itself with the spirit of racism and fiercely opposes efforts aimed at reconciliation.

THE PROBLEM WITH PAIN

There is pain associated with discrimination. If we are not careful we can be so consumed by the pain that it dictates how we view and live our lives. Anyone who has lived on the earth for very long is experienced with the problem of pain. Pain results from anything which causes suffering, distress, agony, anguish, or despair. People who feel like victims hesitate to be spontaneous in the things of God.

 AT A GLANCE

The eighth chapter of Romans gives us some insight into the workings of pain.

DIVINE COUNSEL FOR OUR PAIN		
REFERENCE	THE WORKINGS OF PAIN	GOD'S COUNSEL TO US
Romans 8:1	Pain comes from accusation.	Live according to the Spirit.
Romans 8:18	Pain causes us to be short-sighted.	Look for the glory that will be revealed.
Romans 8:26	Pain obscures the possibilities of hope.	The Holy Spirit ministers to us and through us in prayer.
Romans 8:31	Pain tends to convince us that we are by ourselves.	Realize the presence of God in our lives.

Romans 8:37	Pain causes us to be stopped by undesirable circumstances.	Realize that we are more than conquerors through Jesus.

Jesus once healed a man who had been ill and bedridden for 38 years (John 5:1–15). Perhaps the interesting feature about this incident is that Jesus asked, "Do you want to be made well?

What effect do you think 38 years of helplessness and hopelessness had had on this man's expectations for the future? (John 5:7)

The answer to Jesus' question would seem obvious. Why do you think Jesus asked this man if he wanted to be made well? (John 5:6)

How do you think some people arrive at a point where they become attached to the self-pity or anger that accompanies their sense of being a victim of life or society?

Jesus phrased His question to solicit a "yes" or "no" response (John 5:6). What unasked question did the lame man answer instead? (v. 7)

What does this man's response say about how he felt victimized by unfairness? (John 5:7)

Why do you think Jesus didn't help the bedridden man to his feet? Why did Jesus require him to act on his own? (John 5:8)

What do you think Jesus wants to do for those who feel victimized by life or society? What does He demand of them? Why does He expect more determination and effort of some than others?

The man Jesus healed by the pool didn't know who had healed him until later (John 5:13, 15). Then Jesus warned him not to misuse his new health and liberty from pain (v. 14). Why do you think those Jesus has delivered from pain need to be careful to follow Him and not fall back into a victim mentality?

Responding to the pain felt by a victim is a spiritual task because the pain first and foremost is a pain of the heart. Proverbs 18:14 tells us, "The spirit of a man will sustain him in sickness, but who can bear a broken spirit?"

WORD WEALTH

A broken spirit is one's personhood which has been crushed by life's difficulties. It is often accompanied by depression (Prov. 15:13; 17:22). Healing such wounded personalities is part of Jesus' ministry (Luke 4:18).[1]

THE POWER OF PRAYER

In the middle of one of those dusty, long genealogies in 1 Chronicles, the chronicler introduces for just two verses an intriguing character named Jabez (1 Chr. 4:9, 10). Jabez's father isn't named, and it's been suggested that he may not have been honorable.² Jabez was singled out as the most honorable among his kin. His mother named him Jabez because pain would be his companion in life.

When someone sets out to live a more godly life than anyone in his or her family has for a long time, what problems will he or she face?

What pain does that person invite into his or her experience?

Jabez had a four-part prayer that outlined his goals in life. What were the four things Jabez prayed for? (1 Chr. 1:10)

1.

2.

3.

4.

Who do you know who tends to regard himself or herself as a victim of life?

If you were going to translate the four parts of Jabez's prayer into a prayer for your acquaintance, what specifically would you pray for in each part?

1.

2.

3.

4.

HOPE AND RESTORATION ARE IN JESUS

When men and women become aware that they do not have to remain victims and live in spiritual pain, some will flock to places where they will be accepted and received and will see their potential realized. These people will not all look good and they will bring lots of baggage with them from years of bondage. What will the church do with them?

Believe it or not, David had to decide what to do with a cave full of victims shortly after he escaped King Saul's attempts to murder him.

What kinds of people gathered to David in the cave of Adullam? (1 Sam. 22:2)

Why do you think these people gathered to David and allowed him to be captain over them (1 Sam. 22:2)? What was it about him? Why did they feel comfortable with him?

What do you think would have been the greatest hardships and benefits associated with a large group of people living together in a cave?

- Hardships

- Benefits

Through the remaining chapters of 1 Samuel these men got a chance to see how David lived. His life was an open book before them. What do you think it did for these men as they watch David deal with Saul? (1 Sam. 24:1–22; 26:1–25)

 FAITH ALIVE

These distressed, indebted, and discontented people who gathered to David at the cave of Adullam in later years became David's mighty men (2 Sam. 23:8–21). Association with David, faith in the living God, and experiences of success in His service had transformed despondent victims into assertive heroes.

What do those in our midst who feel like rejected victims of society need to experience in each of these areas to rise above the trap of victimhood?

- Spiritual leadership

- Personal faith in Christ

- Success in their local church

When Peter and John went to the temple to pray in Acts 3, they encountered a lame man at the Beautiful gate of the temple. If there was ever a biblical character who had a right to feel like a victim, this was the guy.

What physical right did this man have to feel like a victim? (Acts 3:2)

What social structures must have added to his sense of hopelessness and worthlessness? (Acts 3:2)

WORD WEALTH

Ask translates a Greek verb which usually describes a suppliant making a request of someone in a higher position, such as an individual asking something from God (Matt. 21:22), a subject from a king (Mark 6:25), a child from a parent (Luke 11:11), or a beggar from a person of substance. The word denotes insistent asking without qualms.[3]

What do you think the lame man's immediate reaction was when Peter told him he wasn't going to give him help from his wallet but help from Jesus? (Acts 3:6)

After being in his condition for so long, the lame man wouldn't have thought about getting up if Peter hadn't grabbed him and pulled him erect (Acts 3:7). The strength wasn't there until Peter reached down and connected with him. How can we make contact with people in our community who feel like victims?

How can we become agents through whom the power of the name of Jesus can restore victims to spiritual strength and hope?

 KINGDOM EXTRA

In general, **name** signifies the term by which a person is called. However, it was quite common both in Hebrew and Hellenistic Greek to use this term for all that the name implies, such as rank or authority, character, or reputation. Occasionally **name** was synonymous with the person himself.[4]

In this first recorded miracle performed by the disciples, we are given the key for use by all believers in exercising faith's authority (Acts 3:1–10). When commanding healing for the lame man, Peter employs the full name/title of our Lord: "Jesus Christ [Messiah] of Nazareth." "Jesus" ("Joshua" or "Yeshua") was a common name among Jews and continues to be in many cultures today. But the declaration of His full name and title, a noteworthy practice in Acts, seems a good and practical lesson for us (see Acts 2:22; 4:10).

Let us be complete when claiming our authority over sickness, disease, or demons. In our confession of faith or proclamation of power, confess His deity and His lordship as the Christ (Messiah); use His precious name, as Jesus (Savior). Call upon Him as Lord Jesus, or Jesus Christ, or Jesus of Nazareth, there being no legal or ritual demand intended in this point. But it is wise to remember, just as we pray "in Jesus' name" (John 16:24), so we exercise all authority in Him—by the privilege of power He has given us in His name (Matt. 28:18; Mark 16:12; John 14:13, 14).[5]

FAITH ALIVE

In some way Peter perceived that the lame man was prepared to put his faith in the name of Jesus (Acts 3:16). What factors may have made him ready to believe in Christ?

What can we do to lay the groundwork for faith in the lives of men and women who feel they are victims?

How might you try to encourage a person on welfare who can't find a way to get off?

How might you try to encourage a person embittered by feelings of being a victim of racial quotas in local hiring practices?

 FAITH ALIVE

When in your life have you felt like a victim of forces or people you had no control over? What spiritual factors do you think operated in that situation?

Could you do much to help yourself as the Lord moved you in that situation or did He have to reach down and lift you up Himself?

At the depths of your unhappiness as a victim, if the Lord had asked you, "Do you want to be made well?" what would you have said? Why?

What "victims" in our culture do you feel the greatest compassion for? How has God equipped you to be a rescuer or an encourager for them?

 FAITH ALIVE

As a result of working through the materials of *Race and Reconciliation: Healing the Wounds, Winning the Harvest,* what is the most important change the Lord has produced in your attitudes toward racial reconciliation?

What is the one thing you would most like to see your church do to advance racial reconciliation as a result of this study?

What is the key thing you think God wants you to commit yourself to do as your part in His ministry of reconciliation?

1. *Spirit-Filled Life® Bible* (Nashville: Thomas Nelson Publishers, 1991), 907-908, note on Prov. 18:14.

2. Jack Hayford, "The Prayer of Jabez, A Fresh Breath of Prayer," Tape 03791 (Van Nuys, CA: Sound Word Tape Ministry).

3. *Spirit-Filled Life® Bible,* 1416, "Word Wealth: Matt. 7:7, ask."

4. Ibid., 1598, "Word Wealth: John 12:13, name."

5. Ibid., 1629, "Kingdom Dynamics: Acts 3:6, Jesus' Name: Faith's Complete Authority."

Appendix 1/The Concept of "Race" in the Bible

"Race" refers to a group of humans possessing character-istics passed down genetically that are sufficiently recognizable for distinguishing between groups. Such characteristics may be physical, including such external and visible features as height, color of hair, kind of hair, and skin pigmentation. Others may be more subtle and involve such matters as blood types (O, A, B, AB). It is unlikely any one individual ever possesses all of the characteristics or traits that mark his or her race.

MISUSING THE BIBLE TO SUPPORT RACISM

Misusing Creation Texts. Although the only reference to "race" in the NKJV is Zechariah 9:6, and the subject of race is not developed in any comprehensive way in the Bible, various passages of Scripture have often been used to promote racial prejudice. Ranging from relatively harmless to extremely vicious, they tend to cluster around the early chapters of Gene-sis. It has been suggested, for example, that the stories of Adam and Eve (Genesis 2—3) apply only to Caucasians. Oth-ers have argued that Cain was the black ancestor of the so-called Negroid stock, a theory that plays into the hands of racists (in the light of Cain's sinful behavior; see Gen. 4:1–15). Still others have proposed the especially reprehensible idea that "(hu)man(kind)" in Genesis 1 refers to members of the Cauca-soid race and that "beasts" in the same chapter refers to mem-bers of the Negroid race, thus giving aid and comfort to those

From "Race," in *Nelson's New Illustrated Bible Dictionary,* Ronald F. Youngblood, Gen. Ed., (Nashville: Thomas Nelson, 1995), 1061–1064.

who might wish to exercise dominion over their fellows since—by definition—"beasts" are sub-human. Needless to say, none of these theories is worthy of adoption—or even consideration—by serious students of Scripture.

Misusing the Curse of Canaan. An equally false theory, however, has unfortunately gained popular belief among some Bible readers. They have understood Noah's curse on Canaan (Gen. 9:25) and his blessing on Shem and Japheth (Gen. 9:26–27) as providing adequate justification for the enslavement of blacks by whites. The theory is usually connected to the possibility that the Hebrew word "Ham" (the father of Canaan) means "black." But the problems with this line of argument are many:

(1) The proper name Ham may very well not mean "black" at all.
(2) Even if it does, Noah's curse is not against Ham but against his son Canaan.
(3) All known peoples grouped under the name of "Canaanites" (descendants of Canaan) were Caucasoid, not Negroid.
(4) Nothing in the text of Genesis 9 indicates that the curse was lasting and could be expected to surface again thousands of years after it was originally uttered.
(5) Noah's prediction that Canaanites would some day be subservient to S(h)emites was adequately fulfilled in, for example, Joshua 9. Because the inhabitants of Gibeon and other cities (Josh. 9:17) had "worked craftily . . . and pretended to be [peace-loving] ambassadors" (Josh. 9:4), Joshua said to them, "You are cursed, and none of you shall be freed from being slaves—woodcutters and water carriers for the house of my God" (Josh. 9:23). In other words, Noah's curse in Genesis 9 was part of the Lord's overall strategy of subduing the land of Canaan under the leadership of Joshua and the armies of Israel.

Misusing other Biblical Passages. In addition, nowhere in the Bible is dark skin a sign of inferior status. Job's skin became black as a result of his illness (Job 30:30). Although the Shulamite is "dark," she is none the less "lovely" (Song 1:5).

Lamentations 5:10 states: "Our skin was black like an oven because of the terrible famine" (KJV). And as far as Jeremiah 13:23 is concerned, John Calvin notes appropriately that "learned men in our age do not wisely refer to this passage when they seek to prove that there is no free will in man; for it is not simply the nature of man that is spoken of here, but the habit that is contracted by long practice." To put it in the vivid imagery of the text itself, it is no more possible for people who are accustomed to doing evil to then suddenly start to do good than it is for an Ethiopian to change his skin color or a leopard to change its spots. Just as there is nothing inherently evil in the color of the leopard's spots, so also there is nothing inherently evil in the color of an Ethiopian's skin—whatever that color might have been. The subject of Jeremiah 13:23 is not skin color but the extreme difficulty of altering ingrained habits.

THE BIBLICAL ORIGIN OF RACES

Simple: Derived from Noah's Three Sons. If the Bible speaks anywhere of the origin of what we would today refer to as "races," it is in Genesis 10 (often called the Table of Nations). In that chapter the people of the Biblical world (basically the eastern Mediterranean basin) are divided on the basis of their descent from one or more of Noah's three sons (Shem, Ham, and Japheth). Since the Hebrew word for "son" can also mean "descendant" or "successor" or even "nation," and since the word "father" can also mean "ancestor" or "predecessor" or even "founder," we should not be surprised that some of the "sons" listed in Genesis 10 are in fact ethnic or tribal groups (see Gen. 10:13–14 and especially 10:16–18).

As it turns out, therefore, the Table of Nations is a kind of literary map of the ancient Near East. The "sons" of Japheth (10:2–4) inhabited the territories north of Canaan and also lived in the maritime regions of southeast Europe. The "sons" of Ham (10:6–19) settled down in Canaan and along the southern shores of the Red Sea (including northeast Africa, notably Egypt). The "sons" of Shem included the Hebrew people (the "children of Eber," 10:21) and other S(h)emitic peoples such as the Assyrians, Arameans and Arabs (10:22–30). They occupied large tracts of territory in western Asia.

Complex: Described from Many Perspectives. It is important to observe that the three main divisions of peoples in the listing of nations (Gen. 10:32) are not always (or only) racial in origin. With respect to the "sons" of Ham, for example, we are told that they were separated out "according to their families, according to their languages, in their lands and in their nations" (10:20; see similarly 10:5, 31). "Families" is an ethnic term, "languages" is a linguistic term, "lands" is geographic, and "nations" is political. It is clear, therefore, that several criteria were used in describing the "ancestry" or location of this or that group of people. This may help to explain why a few of them, such as Sheba (10:7, 28) and Havilah (10:7, 29), are listed more than once. Perhaps, in one case, the division was based on ethnic or linguistic considerations while in another case a geographic or political concern was most important. It is worth noting that skin color and other "racial" characteristics are totally absent from the Table of Nations.

THE BIBLE AND INTERRACIAL UNITY

Racial Intermarriage. Conveniently summarized in the genealogical lists of 1 Chronicles 1, the total of nations is seventy, a number that often symbolizes completion: fourteen from Japheth (1 Chron. 1:5–7), thirty from Ham (1:8–16), and twenty-six from Shem (1:17–23). Before the Israelites occupied Canaan, seven (again, a number signifying completion) groups of people inhabited it: Amorites, Canaanites, Girgashites, Hittites, Hivites, Jebusites, and Perizzites (Deut. 7:1; Josh. 3:10; 24:11). Sometimes the list is reduced to as few as two (Gen. 13:7; 34:30; Judg. 1:4–5) or expanded to as many as ten (Gen. 15:19–21)—another number often symbolizing completion.

Israelites sometimes intermarried with people from one or more of those nations (Gen. 34:2, 9, 16, 21). Since all members of the human race are of the biological species *Homo sapiens,* such intermarriage is not wrong in and of itself. But since marrying into a foreign tribal group implied accepting that group's religion, the people of God were warned not to do so. Indeed, Nehemiah called curses down on a number of Jewish men in his day because they had married women from Ashdod, Ammon, and Moab (Neh. 13:23–25). He reminded them that King Solomon had committed a grave error in this regard: "Pagan women caused even him to sin. Should we then hear of your doing all this great evil, transgressing against our God by marrying pagan women?" (13:26–27). The fact that the women were foreign, or of another racial or ethnic stock, was not the issue. The sin was in marrying someone who was "pagan." In short, no Old Testament text should be interpreted as condoning racial prejudice or declaring any one "race" to be inherently inferior to any other.

Racial Diversity in the Church. The teachings of Jesus and the apostles in the New Testament are equally clear. Christ died to redeem everyone, and the gospel is to be "preached in His name to all nations" (Luke 24:46–47). God loved all the people in the whole world so much that He gave His Son for them (John 3:16). Although in Jesus' day Jews had "no dealings with Samaritans" (John 4:4), He made a special effort to minister to the needs of a Samaritan woman (4:4, 10–26). Christ draws all people to Himself without regard for race or nationality (John 12:32). The distinguishing mark of true disciples is love for every believer, regardless of race or color (John 13:34–35). No ethnic group is inferior to any other (Acts 10:28). All nations have a common origin and constitute a single human family (Acts 17:26). There is no partiality with God (Acts 10:34–35; Rom. 2:11), and we must follow his example (James 2:1).

Diversity in the church, the body of Christ, is part and parcel of its unity (1 Cor. 12:12–20), and each member of Christ's body, however weak or unpresentable, depends on all the others (12:21–27). Our unity in Christ transcends all false distinctions, whether ethnic, social, or sexual (Gal. 3:28). The blood of Christ abolishes any barrier that would tend to pit one group against another (Eph. 2:13–17; Col. 3:9–11). When the redeemed people of God stand before the throne and the Lamb, they will constitute "a great multitude which no one [can] number, of all nations, tribes, peoples, and tongues" (Rev. 7:9).

CHRISTIAN COMMITMENT TO RACIAL RECONCILIATION

Minority racial groups can be brought into the mainstream of public life only if and when groups that are in the majority welcome them to do so. Discrimination against minorities takes away from them the right to own and possess. Segregation takes away from minorities the right to belong. Stereotyping takes away the right to be what they are naturally and culturally. Racist actions spring from racist attitudes, and therefore people of good will on all sides—members of majority and minority groups alike—must rid themselves of every form of racial prejudice, whether blatant or subtle. *Because racism is sinful, it must be rooted out wherever God's people harbor it or find it. It has no place in any community of believers.* It is sanctioned neither by common sense nor by Holy Scripture.

Christians of every racial stock and ethnic groups must learn—and soon—to worship together, to study together, to pray together, to have fellowship together, to live together in peace and harmony. Since we have already been reconciled to God through Christ, we must now get on with the business of becoming reconciled to each other. The same God who has committed to us the message of reconciliation (2 Cor. 5:19) has also given to us the ministry of reconciliation (5:18)—first to Himself, and then to one another. It is not enough for us to love the Lord our God with all our heart and soul and mind and strength. We must also take the second step: We must be willing—indeed, eager—to love our neighbors as we love ourselves (Mark 12:30–31).

Appendix 2/Resources for Reconciliation

A PRACTICAL PLAN FOR ACHIEVING RACIAL RECONCILIATION

Step One: Hold a racial reconciliation service each year. This will give your congregation an annual reminder and opportunity to evaluate your progress. On this day we encourage the members of your church to affirm the clear position of God's Word on racial issues.

Step Two: Form a racial reconciliation task force to educate your congregation on racial issues and take the lead in reconciliation efforts. The resources listed at the end of this article can help give the group a clearer perspective of:

• What racism is and where it comes from

• The history of racism in America

• The biblical position embracing diversity

• What is being done to successfully deal with the problem

A newsletter from the National Association of Evangelicals/National Black Evangelical Association committee, *The Ambassador,* will be sent upon request to your task force to keep them up to date.[1] This will provide a forum for them to ask specific questions about the effort in your community.

Step Three: Plan to use the Racial Reconciliation elements of worship. This will lead your congregation in an appropriate

The materials of this Appendix are reproduced with permission from materials published by a joint effort of the National Association of Evangelicals, the National Black Evangelical Association, and Zondervan Publishing House. Churches may receive a loose copy for reproduction and use by writing to either Association. Their addresses appear at the end of this Appendix.

admission of the problem, confession, and restoration. Use the reproducible artwork enclosed to print your own bulletin insert. The front cover of this brochure can also be used as a poster to alert your congregation of this event.

Step Four: Begin a friendship with an individual of another race and encourage your congregation to do the same

Step Five: Adopt a "sister church" of a different race. Plan joint activities. Hold a joint elder retreat, a men's retreat, women's retreat, family night at a local gymnasium. Occasionally, participate in pulpit exchanges. Invite families from the "sister church" over for a meal, etc.

Step Six: Commit to persistent prayer regarding racial reconciliation and encourage your congregation to do the same.

Step Seven: Adopt a statement on racism similar to the one developed by the NBEA and NAE.

STATEMENT ON PREJUDICE AND RACISM
National Association of Evangelicals
National Black Evangelical Association

January 26–27, 1990

We have gathered as a group of Christians to address the resurgence of racism in the United States. Because of the historical and current context in which we meet, we are addressing primarily the white-black expression of racism: we recognize that other ethnic groups have also experienced oppression based on race.

We affirm the core conviction of our Judeo-Christian heritage: human life is created in God's image. This imago dei is expressed in one human race (Acts 17:26), but that one humanity fully expresses God's image in a wealth of diversity. A few obvious examples of diversity are maleness and femaleness, and colors of skin, eyes and hair. There are more subtle diversities as well. These diversities are not intended to divide humans from one another; rather they are to add to the wonder of life's wholeness as a gift from God.

We affirm another conviction of our Judeo-Christian roots: as a consequence of a fall from the original state, humanity shares a sin nature. One of the marks of this sin nature, prejudice, is distributed among the diverse parts of the whole humanity. This prejudice, rather than allowing celebration of the diversity of our one humanity, causes the holders of prejudice to view those who are different as inferior, When one ethnic group is in a majority or power position, its group prejudices against those who are minorities are often manifested in racism. Racism is a prejudice plus power. Racism is therefore an institutionalized expression of a controlling group's prejudices.

There was diversity of motivation in the establishment of the United States as a nation, but woven throughout its history was a pattern of racism by the white-dominated society that involved the displacement and destruction of one race, the Native Americans, and the enslavement of yet another, the Africans. The historical record of how white Europeans conquered North America by destroying native population and building their new nation's economy on the backs of kidnapped Africans who had been turned into chattel are facts which must be acknowledged and confessed.

Racism is a foundational sin of the United States, fueled by economic greed and the exploitation of human and natural resources. It has corrupted the foundations, institutions and cultural mores of this country. It has prevented formation of a true cultural democracy. Racism has enslaved, impoverished, and oppressed people of color in America.

The concept of race must be seen as the sum total of what is known as the physical, psychological characteristics that set one group apart from another. These distinctions are not seen as absolutes since it can be readily observed that some basic characteristics thought to be unique to one group and often observed as part of the make-up of another. This leads us to conclude that the racial group in its make-up can be absolutely separated from another. These points on race must lead us to the repudiation of any and all myths concerning the inferiority of African-Americans, such as: they are by nature childlike, that they came from the poorer stock of Africa, and that they gladly gave up their own history and traditions to embrace the "superior" culture of their masters.

To appreciate the scope of sin against African-Americans, it is essential to understand the following points of history:

1. The European Slave Trade began in 1444 A.D. and continued infamously into the late 1800s. However, through the early 1600's there were many blacks who came to America as indentured servants, and who, after their service, were instrumental in building many early settlements. They lost their freedom when slave traders and businessmen had colonial laws changed to accommodate economic considerations.

2. The recurrent history of America's sin of racism is the sting of continual promises, modest gains, followed by a reversal of those gains which has resulted in entrenched prejudicial attitudes and continued economic disenfranchisement for African Americans. The political gains of the 1860s and 70s were instantaneously halted because of white fear, resulting in the inactment of Jim Crow laws that dehumanized African people in poverty and ignorance. Even today, just twenty-five years after the civil rights movement of the 1960s, white American racism is flexing its economic muscle against the African American community and rolling back the positive effects of Affirmative Action.

It must be acknowledged that large segments of Christianity in America have historically been allied with racist institutions and attitudes. Racism attacks the core of the gospel message. It negates the reason for which Christ died. It also denies the purpose of the church: to bring together, in Christ, those who have been divided from one another. Racism has caused many Christians in American to use the Bible to defend segregation, and abandon justice.

Racism is a severe and current sin. It is an idolatry which makes God in the image of the controlling group and uses God to justify willful and/or unintended evil against minority interest. The soul of the nation is under judgment for the talent drain of potential leaders and for the psychological scarring of young blacks who are born in the ghetto but rarely have the opportunity to develop. Racism has historically hindered us from benefiting from the fullness of God's gift to the nation, which is embodied in what is gained from all the people.

The Psalmist asks, "When the foundations are destroyed, what can the righteous do?" The righteous can fill the leadership vacuum by repenting individually and corporately. It will be necessary to re-educate white evangelicalism into understanding that the pioneer black church has held one of the few authentic expressions of the Gospel in America by holding fast to the conviction that God, through His word, was the authority in all matters of life; that all humanity was created in God's image; and that humanity had eternal value evidenced by Christ's inclusive death on the cross.

Although prejudice is a universal sin infecting all peoples, racism in America is basically a white problem. Whites established practices, systems, and laws which entrenched racism, and in some instances, still perpetuate it. Confession and repentance are essential starting points for the correction of any sinful past and they are needed now in America if the rising tide of racism is to be turned back.

The black evangelical church, for its part, must commit itself to constructive protest of racism. This should be combined with a readiness to forgive past wrongs. The black church must help blacks to regain a healthy sense of pride in their identity. The Lordship of Christ must be brought to bear on the life of the black community as well as that of the white community. Economic discipline and investment in the black community, inspired by a spiritual rebirth of the black masses, will be the salvific hope of black America. We affirm that Salvation is in and by Jesus Christ alone. The Gospel of love is transmitted through an inseparable package of faith and action. In and through him we have hope for the life that is and that which is to come.

The white evangelical church must first repent of the sin of racism. It must examine its doctrine, policies, institutions, boards, agencies, and para-church entities and remove any vestiges of prejudice and racism. It must also enter into a meaningful dialogue with black evangelical leaders by means of establishing cultural exchanges on racism in the white community. Most importantly, it must exert pressure for economic justice by witnessing within its own power structures. It must remove the institutional barriers which hinder progress for blacks and other people of color. It must work to make restitution and repair as soon as possible.

As persons redeemed by the atoning work of Christ, we commit ourselves to renewed efforts toward reconciliation and harmony between people of diverse races. Together the entire evangelical community must and can reaffirm the wonderful ethnic diversity among the body of Christ, while at the same time strengthening its unity. The credible witness of the Church and perhaps the deliverance of the United States depends upon the joint evangelical community effort to dismantle the structure of racism and prejudice. Together, we can create a community that will be a monumental witness for Christ in modern times.

We go from this consultation determined to translate these intentions into actions which will exemplify among human kind Christ's reconciling work.

RACIAL RECONCILIATION

WORSHIP GUIDE

*"I have a dream my four little children will one
day live in a nation where they will not be judged by the
color of their skin but by content of their character."*
—*Dr. Martin Luther King, Jr.*

SCRIPTURE READING

Reader: But God demonstrates his own love for us in this:
While we were still sinners, Christ died for us.

Congregation: **Since we have now been justified by his
blood, how much more shall we be saved from God's
wrath through him! For if, when we were God's enemies,
we were reconciled to him through the death of his Son,
how much more, having been reconciled, shall we be saved
through his life! Not only is this so, but we also rejoice in
God through our Lord Jesus Christ, through whom we
have received reconciliation.**

Reader: For he himself is our peace, who has made the
two one and has destroyed the barrier, the dividing wall of
hostility by abolishing in his flesh the law with its commandments and regulations. His purpose was to create in himself
our new man out of the two, thus making peace, and in this
one body to reconcile both of them to God through the cross,
by which he put to death this hostility.

Congregation: **In him the whole building is joined
together and rises to become a holy temple in the Lord.
And in him you too are becoming a dwelling in which
God lives by his Spirit.**

Reader: Therefore, if anyone is in Christ, he is a new creation; the old has gone, the new has come! All this is from
God, who reconciled us to himself through Christ and gave us
the ministry of reconciliation: that God was reconciling the
world to himself in Christ, not counting men's sins against
them. And he has committed to us the message of reconcilia-

(Rom. 5:8–11; Eph. 2:14–16, 21, 22; 2 Cor. 5:17–21; Matt. 5:23, 24 New Interna-
tional Version)

tion. We are therefore Christ's ambassadors, as though God were making his appeal through us. We implore you on Christ's behalf; be reconciled to God. God made him who had no sin to be sin for us, so that in him we might become the righteousness of God.

Congregation: Jesus said . . . "**If you are offering your gift at the altar and there remember that your brother has something against you, leave your gift there in front of the altar. First go and be reconciled to your brother; then come and offer your gift.**"

Prayer of Racial Reconciliation

Father in heaven, we praise and thank you for your wonderful gift of life, as we acknowledge you, the one Creator and Father of all human life. We thank you for the beautiful diversity with which you have blessed us, with such a multitude of talents and gifts.

We do confess, Father, that we have sinned against you in our unwillingness to come together as one body in Jesus Christ. We ask you to forgive us our sins of prejudice and racism, which have denied your blessed name before the world, hindered the purpose of the church, and deeply hurt our brothers and sisters in Christ.

It is only with your strength that we can be the community of believers you would have us be. Blessed Holy Spirit, empower us to commit ourselves to reconciliation and harmony with other believers, that the word of peace and reconciliation through Christ can spread. Grand that we will be living witnesses to the love and peace which make all people one in Christ Jesus our Lord. May the mind of Christ truly be in us that we may live and walk in his peace, holding one another in his love, and modeling his commitment to unity.

We ask this in the name of our Lord Jesus Christ, the Head of his body the Church. Amen.

After this prayer, we suggest a time of personal and corporate confession of racial sins and a time of commitment to "make every effort to keep the unity of the Spirit" (Ephesians 4:3).

BATTLE HYMN OF THE REPUBLIC

Mine eyes have seen the glory of the coming of the Lord,
He is trampling out the vintage where the grapes of Wrath are stored;
He hath loosed the fateful lightning of His terrible swift sword,
His truth is marching on.
I have seen Him in the watch-fires of a hundred circling camps.
They have builded Him an altar in the evening dews and damps;
I can read His righteous sentence by the dim and flaring lamps.
His day is marching on.
He has sounded forth the trumpet that shall never call retreat,
He is sifting out the hearts of men before His judgment seat;
O be swift, my soul, to answer Him, be jubilant, my feet!
Our God is marching on.
In the beauty of the lilies Christ was born across the sea,
With a glory in His being that transfigures you and me;
As He died to make men holy, let us live to make men free!
While God is marching on.
Chorus: Glory! Glory! Hallelujah!
Glory! Glory! Hallelujah!
Glory! Glory! Hallelujah!
His truth is marching on!

For more information contact:

National Black Evangelical Association
P.O. Box 17122
Portland, OR 97217
Ph. 503-285-8028

National Association of Evangelicals
450 Gundersen Drive
Carol Stream, IL 60188
Ph. 708-665-0500

SPIRIT-FILLED LIFE® BIBLE DISCOVERY GUIDE SERIES

* In preparation.

SPIRIT-FILLED LIFE® KINGDOM DYNAMICS
STUDY GUIDE SERIES